Okinawan Karate

The Teachings of Eihachi Ota

by
Michael Rovens
and
Mark Polland

P.O. Box 491788, Los Angeles, CA 90049

Please note that the author and publisher of this book are not responsible in any manner whatsoever for any injury that may result from practicing the techniques and/or following the instructions given within. Because the physical activities described herein may be too strenuous in nature for some readers to engage in safely,

First published in 2006 by Empire Books
Copyright© 2006 by Empire Books, Inc.
All rights reserved. No part of this publication may be reproduced or ultilized in any form or by any means, electronic or mechanical, including photocopying, recording or by any information storage and retrieval system, without prior written permission from Empire Books

Library of Congress: 2003026643
ISBN-10: 1-933901-05-5
ISBN-13: 978-1-933901-05-3

Library of Congress Cataloging-in-Publication Data

Rovens, Michael, 1962-
Okinawan karate : the teachings of Master Eihachi Ota / by Michael Rovens and Mark Polland. -- 1st ed.
p. cm.
ISBN 1-933901-05-5 (pbk. : alk. paper)
1. Karate--Japan--Okinawa-ken.   I. Polland, Mark, 1964-   .
II. Ota, Eihachi. III. Title.
GV1114.3.R68 2004
796.815'3--dc22

2003026643

Empire Books
P.O. Box 491788
Los Angeles, CA 90049
(818) 767-9000

06 05 04 03 02 01 00 99 98 97 1 3 5 7 9 10 8 6 4 2

Printed in the United States of America

Design: Willy Blumhoff

Dedication

This book is dedicated to the memory of my teacher, Grandmaster Shoshin Nagamine, Hanshi 10th–degree black belt and the founder of the Matsubayashi Shorin-ryu style of karate-do. It is my sincere hope that this work will help to describe the genius and elegant beauty of Matsubayashi-ryu. It is also my sincere desire that this work will help to preserve the rich legacy left behind by Grandmaster Nagamine.

Sensei Ota paying his respects at the gravesite of Grandmaster Nagamine.

Contents

Section One: LINEAGE

    Chapter 1:   Lineage............................ 15

    Chapter 2:   Sensei Ota 31

Section Two: KATA

    Chapter 3:   Kata 39

    Chapter 4:   Fukyukata I 59

    Chapter 5:   Fukyukata II....................... 67

    Chapter 6:   Pinan Kata 75

                  I.   Pinan Shodan 79

                  II. Pinan Nidan..................... 87

                  III. Pinan Sandan 93

                  IV. Pinan Yondan 101

                  V. Pinan Godan 109

Chapter 7: Naihanchi Kata 115
             I. Naihanchi Shodan 117
             II. Naihanchi Nidan 123
             III. Naihanchi Sandan 129
Chapter 8: Ananku 135
Chapter 9: Wankan 143
Chapter 10: Rohai 155
Chapter 11: Wanshu 167
Chapter 12: Passai 177
Chapter 13: Gojushiho 191
Chapter 14: Chinto 205
Chapter 15: Kusanku 219

Section Three: TRAINING
Chapter 16: Ikken Hisatsu 237
Chapter 17: Tsumasaki Geri 249
Chapter 18: Kumite 257

Section Four: KOBUDO
Chapter 19: Kobudo 269
Chapter 20: Kama 277
             Kuro-Matsu No-Nicho Kama 289
Chapter 21: Bo 299
Chapter 22: Tonfa 307

Summary 316
About the Authors 318

Acknowledgements

Masao Shima: I would like to thank Master Shima for his ongoing support and encouragement over the past 35 years. Master Shima is the one who promoted me to eighth–degree black belt following Master Nagamine's death. He has been a constant source of inspiration. This has provided me with the fortitude to tackle the enormous undertaking of completing such a comprehensive project as this text.

Kazuo Tajima: I would like to give special thanks to Mr. Tajima for his willingness to act as my liason to Okinawa. In my absense, he was our collector of information and research and the principal communicator to Okinawa of our goals for building our style in the West. Mr. Tajima is one of Master Kishaba's most advanced disciples.

Michael Rovens: Perhaps more than any other, Michael deserves my thanks and congratulations. It was Michael's idea to begin this project and his determination which facilitated its completion. Michael accompanied me on two research sabbaticals to
Okinawa. He also was the principal author who set my thoughts and theories to paper, hopefully in a way which will

be easily understood by readers and fellow practitioners. In addition, he supervised the photographic effort and the computer layout in total, a task which took more than five years to complete.

Siamack Karimi: Pictured on the left following class at the Shinzato dojo. I would like to thank "Sia" for his ongoing support of this project. He too accompanied me on two research excursions to Okinawa. His technical and computer skills were an enormous benefit in completing this task.

Mark Polland: Mark also deserves my special thanks for his years of support and hard work at the dojo, and for the co-writing and organization of the book and the editing of the text.

Acknowlegements

Don Warrener: Mr. Warrener has trained for more than 30 years in Goju-ryu. Mr. Warrener owns a publishing company and was the person responsible for producing my introductory video tapes that were released in 1999. Mr. Warrener selflessly spent hours shooting the photographs which appear in this text.

Evan Ziegeweid: I would like to thank Evan for the countless hours he spent finishing the photographs in Adobe Photoshop.

Preface

In writing this book, the authors were cognizant of the fact that certain words used in the text are Japanese; therefore they would be unfamiliar to some readers. Though we have not defined every Japanese word, we have attempted to provide basic definitions for the words that are the most important in the context of this book, and for those which we thought might be the least familiar to our readers.

For words that are not commonly part of the English language, we have adopted the Japanese word, as well as the Japanese usage. For example, the word "kata" is a Japanese word that means "form" or "forms" and is used to refer to the preset exercise routine(s) that karate practitioners use for training. The word kata is used to express both the singular and plural form of the noun, like the English words "deer" or "fish." We have elected not to alter the original Japanese by adding "s" onto the end of the word to indicate the plural. Consequently, in keeping with the Japanese tradition, in this book the word kata is used as either the singular or plural depending on context, as are the words "Fukyukata," "Pinan," and "Nahanchi." For example, the word Pinan can refer either to all five Pinan kata collectively or simply to one of the five forms.

The authors have attempted to remain faithful to the Japanese in this regard, both out of respect for the culture from which the word derives, and in an effort to preserve the

Preface

nuances of the original, even if only in some small way. Although this usage may sound unfamiliar to some readers, our feeling is that it is preferable to maintain the spirit of the original by adapting our language to the concepts embodied in the cultural traditions from which karate was developed, rather than corrupting the original to conform to our, admittedly foreign sensibilities.

To paraphrase the title of Grandmaster Nagamine's book, *The Essence of Karate-do*, which was in large part the inspiration for this book, it is the essence of karate that we are trying to convey. By using the Japanese words in keeping with their tradition, we believe that the text better preserves the flavor of the culture from which it comes. We are more concerned about carrying on the essence of this distinctively Japanese art form than in perpetuating the linguistic conventions handed down to us by the Old English and Ancient Roman peoples half a world away.

In contrast, the reader will note that proper names of persons are written according to the European convention. The given name is listed first, and the family or surname is listed afterward. Unlike many other texts, in this book the European convention is used with all names, regardless of whether the person has an Asian or European name. In keeping with that European convention, we have also placed titles, such as Sensei or Master, before the person's proper name, rather than afterwards, as it would be used in Japanese.

While we recognize that these practices are not in keeping with proper Japanese, we believe that it adds clarity, especially since the book was written in English and we expect our readers to be familiar with English usage. Though this may seem somewhat inconsistent with our earlier insistence on preserving the traditional usage of Japanese words by not adding "s" on the end to indicate the plural, we decided that the arrangement of the words was an adaptation we were willing to make for the sake of clarity, whereas changing the actual Japanese words was not.

We hope that our readers, whatever their cultural and linguistic origins, forgive us for these "trespasses" and understand that they were made for the sake of clarity and integrity and nothing more.

Note on the Kata Photographs

Although the sections on kata are comprehensive insofar as every kata in the Matsubayashi Shorin-ryu curriculum is covered, these sections are not intended to be instructional guides for students to learn new kata.

Rather than trying to teach students these kata, our purpose here is to convey some of the insight that Sensei Ota, a Master of the art, has learned through his lifetime of experience. To that end, we were not concerned with explaining such things as the proper height for a chest punch or the proper angle for a shuto. We leave those issues to the individual practitioners and their instructors.

Our intention is to comment on movements and techniques which apply to the body mechanics Sensei Ota teaches. At times, we have commented on points of strategy, but only where it relates to Sensei Ota's philosophy regarding combat situations.

With that in mind, the reader will note that in the following chapters on kata there are extended passages of photographs, sometimes with very little commentary. This is not because those moves are unimportant, but because the execution of these movements does not relate directly to the body mechanics that we have covered in this book.

When we have commented on fundamentals which apply in the beginning kata and then are repeated in ensuing kata, we don't make the comment every time but rather the first time the movement occurs.

Section One
LINEAGE

Grandmaster Nagamine

1
Lineage

Grandmaster Shoshin Nagamine, a 10th–degree black belt, is the founder of the Matsubayashi Shorin-ryu style of karate. During his lifetime, the Okinawan government declared Nagamine an intangible cultural treasure because of the rich legacy he established and because of the important position he holds in the history of the art of karate. Nagamine studied karate under several of the most famous masters of all times, including Ankichi Arakaki, Kodatsu Iha, Chotoku Kyan and Choki Motobu. These earlier masters that Nagamine studied with either studied directly or once removed from two of the most prominent figures in the history of Okinawan karate: Soken Matsumura, one of the original founders of Shuri-te, and Kosaku Matsumora, one of the original stalwarts of Tomari-te. In *The Essence of Okinawan Karate-do,* Nagamine states that his ideas are based upon the teachings of these two notable karate legends. In 1947, Nagamine decided to adopt the name of Matsubayshi-ryu for his style of karate, in honor of both Matsumura of Shuri and Matsumora of Tomari. In this way, Nagamine expounds, "The names of these masters are retained forever in our minds."

Tomari-te is sometimes referred to by historians as the lost art of karate because there are no pure Tomari-te styles which are still in existence today. However, Tomari-te also included many techniques common to Shuri-te. The experts from both villages were well known in their respective communities and were certainly well known to each other. For the most part, the traditions of Tomari-te were ultimately absorbed into the Shuri-te styles.

Matsubayashi Shorin-ryu is one of the few hybrid styles which still preserves these ancient Tomari-te traditions. Grandmaster Nagamine's teachers who practiced and passed on those Tomari-te traditions include: Kodatsu Iha, who was the top student of Kosaku Matsumora of Tomari; Choki Motobu, who in addition to learning from Itosu, also studied with Matsumora of Tomari; and Chotoku Kyan, who studied with Kokan Oyadomari, the other prominent Tomari-te expert besides Matsumora.

There are only three extant Tomari-te kata: Wankan, Rohai and Wanshu. Each of these kata are integral to the Matsubayashi-ryu kata curriculum. Even Passai and Chinto kata reflect the strong Tomari-te influence in Matsubayashi-ryu. One of the most significant aspects of Nagamine's Matsubayashi-ryu style of karate is that it preserves the body mechanics that are unique to Tomari-te. Many Tomari-te kata actually originated around the Shuri district of Okinawa and later migrated to Tomari where the forms were changed to reflect the body mechanics unique to the Tomari district. Tomari-te movements can be characterized as light and quick. The emphasis was on snapping combinations rather than on one powerful blow.

The remainder of this chapter is an attempt to trace the roots of Matsubayashi-ryu from its namesakes to the men who are still preserving the lineage. Understanding the evolution of this lineage not only lends credibility to the successors of the style, but helps differentiate the unique body mechanics which make Matsubayashi-ryu so culturally important to the world of Okinawan karate.

Chapter 1 — Lineage

THE FOREFATHERS

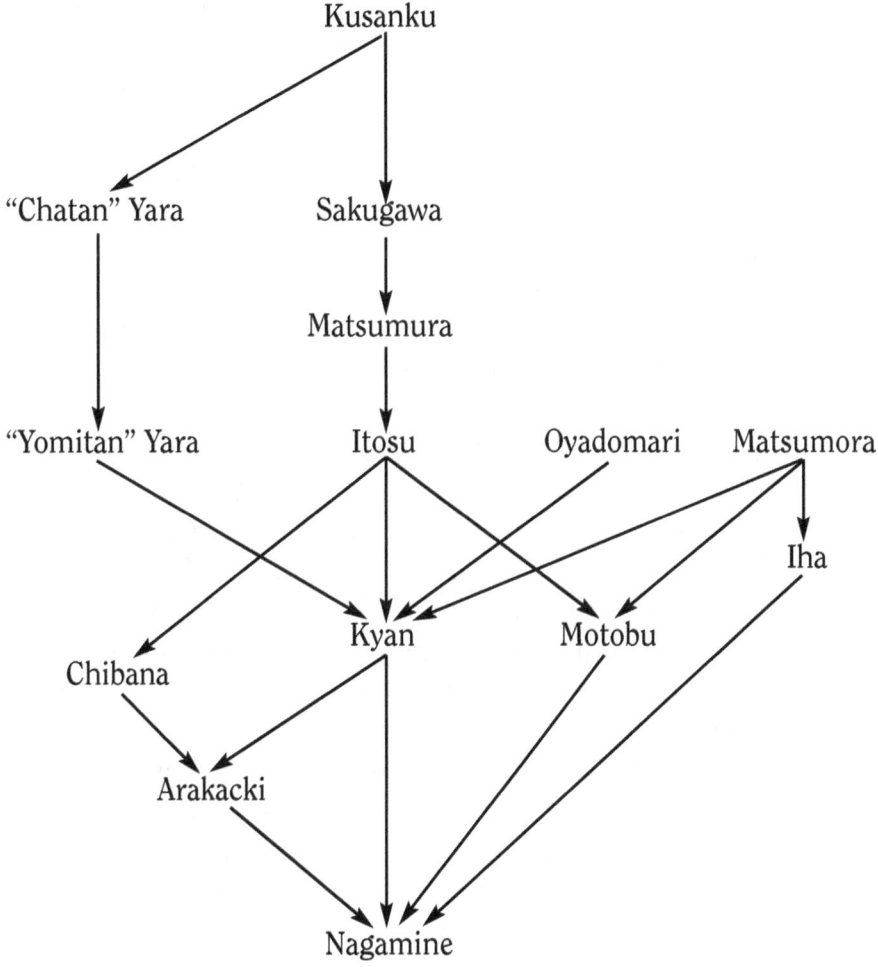

NAGAMINE'S TEACHERS' TEACHERS (1st generation)

Sokon "Bushi' Matsumura (1809–1901)

Matsumura studied with the great "To-de" or "Chinese hand" Sakugawa. That name suggests that Sakugawa taught Chinese martial arts, not Okinawan-te, or he would have been referred to as "Te' Sakugawa. Nagamine explains that this title meant that Sakugawa was an expert in Chinese style martial arts. Other traditions purport that Matsumura's teacher was Choken "the Birdman" Makabe (1769-1825), perhaps a senior student of Sakugawa, and a legendary practitioner in the karate history of Shuri and Tomari. Yet, in *Tales of Okinawa's Great Masters*, Nagamine has Makabe as pre-dating Sakugawa in karate history. Additionally, Matsumura also studied with the Chinese military envoy, Kusanku. Matsumura also traveled to China to further his studies, where he met the famous Iwah. Matsumura is also believed to have mastered the art of Jigen-ryu, a style of Kenjutsu (sword fighting), while stationed in Satsuma Prefecture. Nagamine describes Matsumura as successfully reinterpreting the indigenous Okinawan-te by applying the principles of Chuan fa (Chinese style martial arts) and Jigen-ryu Kenjutsu.

Matsumura is credited with either creating or passing down the kata Kusanku. He is also credited with the kata Passai, Naihanchi I-II, Chinto, Gojushiho and Hakutsuru. Matsumura became the head bodyguard for the Royal Okinawan family. His most important student was Itosu, but he named his grandson, Nabe Matsumura, as his successor. Later, Nabe Matsumura appointed his nephew, Hohan Soken, as his successor. Grandmaster Soken named the style Matsumura Orthodox. Matsumura, like Sensei Ota, believed that developing speed in every technique was the key to developing power. Matsumura also was a pioneer in using hip rotation as a way to develop power in technique.

Yara (1740–1812)

Chatan Yara or Yara from Chatan village was a student of Kusanku and a contemporary of To-de Sakugawa. He supposedly passed on a version of the kata Kusanku, known today as Yara Kusanku. However, the person most responsible for passing this form on to modern practitioners was Yomitan Yara, or Yara of Yomitan village. He was born in 1816 and was the grandson of Chatan Yara. Yomitan Yara taught Kusanku kata to Chotoku Kyan. Nagamine states that Yomitan Yara was younger than Sokon Matsumura, but not his inferior in karate. Yara was reknowned for his agility, but his strength was in decline by the time Kyan studied with him.

Anko Itosu (1831–1915)

Yasutsune Itosu was born in Shuri. His nickname was "Anko" which means "Iron Horse." The nickname was given to Itosu because of the way he rooted himself to the ground when practicing kata. An educated man, Itosu was largely responsible for the introduction of karate into the Okinawa public school system. Itosu was the top student of Sokon Matsumura and was largely responsible for preserving Matsumura's kata. Itosu also created many kata himself, including Pinan and Naihanchi sandan. He supposedly created the popular version of Kusanku by combining the Yara and Sakugawa/Matsumura versions together. One of the most remarkable contributions of Itosu was the number of great karatemen he trained, including: Kentsu Yabu, Chomo Hanashiro, Gichin Funakoshi (the founder of Shotokan), Kenwa Mabuni (the founder of Shito-ryu), Chotoku Kyan, Choki Motobu, Yabiku Moden (the teacher of Shinken Taira), Chosin Chibana (the founder of Kobayashi-ryu),

Shimpan Gusukuma, and Chojo Oshiro (reknowned practitioner of Yamane-ryu).

Kosaku Matsumora (1829–1898)

Matsumora studied under two very prominent Tomari-te masters, including Giko Uku and Kishin Teruya. But the most famous is the story of an unnamed Chinese man who was shipwrecked near the port of Tomari and lived in a cave, near Master Teruya's family tomb. Matsumora discovered that the man was an expert in Chinese martial arts. Apparently, after showing great persistence, the Chinese teacher finally accepted Matsumora as a student. This man is remembered for his light footwork and quick, snapping techniques. One day the man disappeared mysteriously, but he left his mark on great karatemen like Kosaku Matsumora and Anko Itosu. This story is important because it further illustrates the connection between Shuri-te (Itosu) and Tomari-te (Matsumora) practitioners. Nagamine recounts a story of Matsumora, in *Tales of Okinawa's Great Masters,* of Matsumora defeating a Satsuma samurai by using a wet towel wrapped around rocks. During the fight, Matsumora lost a finger. Yet, despite this handicap, he became an expert at staff fighting.

Matsumora also studied under Chatan Yara. According to Grandmaster Nagamine, Matsumora learned Naihanchi from Uku, and Passai and Wanshu from Teruya. Teruya's favorite kata was Wanshu. Matsumora's top student was Kodatsu Iha, but he also taught Choki Motobu. Indeed, one of Motobu's few defeats in a streetfight came at the hands of Iha. Matsumora taught Motobu Naihanchi and Passai kata. Several genealogies also list Matsumora as a teacher of Chotoku Kyan.

Kokan Oyadomari (1831–1905)

The other great Tomari-te genealogy traces its lineage back to Kokan Oyadomari. Oyadomari was the other major teacher of Chotoku Kyan. Although not given the same distinction by Nagamine as an influence upon the Matsubayashi-ryu style as Matsumora, Oyadomari's contributions, nonetheless, had an important impact on karatemen from Tomari.

NAGAMINE'S INSTRUCTORS (2nd generation)

Kodatsu Iha (1873–1928)

Kodatsu Iha was the top disciple of Kokan Matsumora of Tomari. While Nagamine was a senior in high school, he studied under Iha at the Tomari Student Association. Nagamine remembers Iha as a very strict instructor but still a very kind man. Much of the Tomari-te heritage passed through Iha and on to Masters like Nagamine. Nagamine learned the Tomari versions of Passai, Chinto, Wankan, Rohai and Wanshu kata directly from Iha and has preserved these forms in his Matsubayashi-ryu style.

Chotoku Kyan (1870–1945)

Chotoku Kyan descended from royalty. His father was well respected as a scholar and a warrior. Kyan was perhaps Nagamine's most important teacher and perhaps better than any modern figure represents the integration of both Shuri-te and Tomari-te. Kyan studied directly from Sokon Matsumura of Shuri and from his top disciple, Anko Itosu. He also studied from Kokan Oyadomari, the other karate great from Tomari. Some genealogies also have Kyan as a student of Kosaku Matsumora. It was from Maeda Peichin, one of Matsumora's top students, that Kyan learned the kata Wanshu. Kyan also learned a version of the kata Kusanku from Yara of Yomitan village.

Grandmaster Nagamine describes Kyan as very small in stature. Consequently, Nagamine credits Kyan with developing a strategy that allowed him to avoid an attack, but never having to back up when evading. Instead, Kyan always moved forward or sideways to evade and then countered with a devastating counterattack. Kyan is also credited with developing a special jodan-zuki or upper block. Chotoku Kyan is remembered as one of the finest technicians ever. Nagamine trained with Kyan at the Kadena Police station where he studied Passai, Chinto and Kusanku (Yomitan Yara version).

Choki Motobu (1871–1949)

Although Motobu is best remembered for his skill in kumite and as a streetfighter, his kata was also exceptional. Nevertheless, Motobu believed that the applications of kata had their limits; they were not intended to be used against professional fighters or in combat situations. Motobu knew from experience that no two street encounters are ever the same. But kata never varies.

Motobu came from a well known aristocratic family, but he was never allowed to learn his family's style of karate (Motobu-ryu) because it was passed down only to the eldest son. Nonetheless, he became one of the toughest fighters in Okinawa, largely on his own and through determined effort. For this reason, Sensei Ota feels a close connection to Motobu. Grandmaster Nagamine, in *Tales of Okinawa's Great-Masters*, asserts that despite Motobu's lack of formal training, aptitude and determination make up for a lot, and Motobu had plenty of both.

Motobu studied both Shuri-te with Itosu and Tokumine and Tomari-te with Matsumora. Nagamine describes Motobu as having attached great importance to makiwara practice. His specialty was the forefinger-knuckle punch. Motobu believed that if a practitioner understood the defensive themes and corresponding application principals of kata, knowing just a few forms was more than enough. It was Tokumine (also known for his penchant in bojutsu) who tought Motobu how to apply his skill. Motobu often expounded the importance of understanding the distance between a practitioner and opponent.

Chapter 1 — Lineage

Ankichi Arakacki (1899–1927)

Arakacki began his study of karate under Shimpan Gusukuma (1890-1954) and Chomo Hanashiro (1869-1945). Both were extraordinary karatemen who studied under Anko Itosu of Shuri. Later Arakacki studied kata under Chosin Chibana, the founder of Kobayashi Shorin-ryu, and body mechanics under Chotoku Kyan, the founder of Shobayashi Shorin-ryu. Arakacki was one of Nagamine's most important teachers. Nagamine describes Arakacki as specializing in waza or technique. Nagamine credits Arakacki with inventing tsumasaki-geri, a toe-tip kick to penetrate vital areas of the body. He even defeated a sumo wrestler with this powerful and lethal technique. The toe-tip kick is also a favorite technique of Sensei Ota.

THE SUCCESSORS

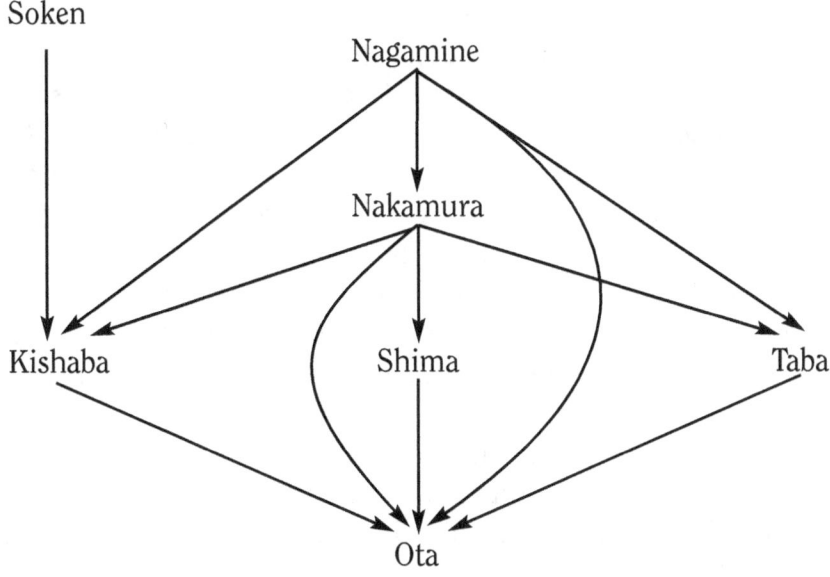

NAGAMINE'S STUDENTS
(4th generation)

Kata Training: Shima front left, Taba front right

L to R: Shima, Kina, Taba, Kishaba

Masao Shima (1933 – 2003)

Master Shima was born September 15, 1933, in the Uenokura district of Naha City. He began his study of karate in 1949, when he was sixteen years old. His father was close personal friends with Grandmaster Nagamine and enrolled his son in the Nagamine dojo. Master Shima remembers Nagamine as a very hard, strict teacher. In those days, Masters like Nagamine only instructed students that displayed the proper character. This was especially important to Nagamine, Shima recalls, because at the time Nagamine was chief of police in Motobu City. Master Shima remembers that training at the Nagamine dojo was mostly kata practice with small emphasis spent on pre-arranged kumite practice. Today, Master Shima explains a much greater emphasis is placed upon free sparring practice.

Students of Master Shima remember him to be one of the hardest teachers in Okinawa. Students tease that he was a masochist because his practice sessions were so severe. Sometimes he was teasingly referred to as "the devil' by seniors

Chapter 1 — Lineage

in the dojo because of how hard he drove his students. When Master Shima opened his dojo, there were only six dojo altogether in Naha: Shoshin Nagamine (Matsubayashi-ryu), Masao Shima (Matsubayashi-ryu), Yuchoku Higa (Kobayashi-ryu), Eichi Miyazato (Goju-ryu), Meitoku Yagi (Goju-ryu), and Seiko Itokazu (Uechi-ryu). Today there are dozens of dojo in Naha City with as many styles and organizations represented. One of the primary reasons for opening his dojo, Master Shima recalls, was so that he could practice more kumite. His dojo always enjoyed the reputation as being one of the roughest in Naha. Often, other senior Matsubayashi-ryu instructors like Kensai Taba and Chokei Kishaba would train and teach at the Shima dojo.

Today Master Shima holds the rank of ninth-degree black belt in Matsubayashi-ryu. He is the most senior living practitioner of that style. His favorite kata is Rohai, which he explains is best for practitioners with a lighter and smaller body frame. Rohai is a short kata, but requires a great deal of speed. His favorite weapons are bo and nunchaku. Shima always emphasizes practicing on the makiwara. Master Shima tells students to always "respect" the makiwara, because it helps teach lessons that are invaluable.

Master Shima

At the Shima dojo, classes were held two to three times a day, six days a week. Master Shima, however, remembers how Ota and his senior instructor, Sempai Nohara, would train harder than any of the other students. They always came early and were always the last to leave. According to Shima, they both drove each other and that in turn helped inspire the other students. Sensei Ota recalls that whoever made it to the dojo and started 10 minutes before the other would motivate the other to train even harder during practice. Each day one of them would come a little earlier, and the next day the other would come even earlier than that, to the point that they were almost living at the dojo.

Sensei Ota and Master Shima

Chokei Kishaba (1929–2000)

Master Kishaba was born on October 4, 1929, in the Tomari district of Naha City. He began his study of karate at age 22 with Grandmaster Nagamine. Master Kishaba chose Grandmaster Nagamine's dojo because he felt Shorin-ryu was very beautiful. At the time, the style was tought in few dojo. When he was 33 years old, Master Kishaba began to study with his second teacher, the legendary Grandmaster Hohan Soken.

Master Kishaba created his own system of Shorin-ryu called Kishaba-juku, which focuses on his well known "koshi' technique. Koshi is sometimes translated as "the hips" in English. However, Master Kishaba explains that Koshi is actually the area of the body which also encompasses part of the abdomen. In this way, the technique incorporates "ki," similar to the way ki is manipulated in Tai Chi. Master Kishaba was regarded as one of the most powerful technicians in Okinawa. Seigi Nakamura, Grandmaster Nagamine's senior instructor, had a strong influence on the young Kishaba and was extremely instrumental in helping Kishaba develop his koshi technique. Nakamura moved very quickly and his techniques had explosive impact, which made a strong and lasting impression on Master Kishaba.

Chapter 1 — Lineage

Grandmaster Soken and Master Kishaba

Master Kishaba's favorite kata were Passai, Rohai and Wankan. He also learned a version of Kusanku from Grandmaster Soken that Nagamine later expressed an interest in learning from Kishaba. Master Kishaba's favorite weapons were the sai, kama and bo. He learned kobudo from Grandmaster Soken. However, his younger brother, Master Chogi Kishaba, the headmaster of the Yamane-ryu Bojutsu tradition, also had a tremendous influence on his older brother. Like Master Shima, Master Kishaba is reknowned for his prowess as it applies to combat situations.

Master Kishaba said that Sensei Ota is one of the most talented practitioners of Shorin-ryu. He remembers Ota as very shy and quiet, but perhaps one of the most serious students ever. He recalls the extra

Master Kishaba and Sensei Ota

27

practice Ota used to devote inside and outside the dojo, and relates that Sensei Ota was one of the hardest working students he ever had.

Kensai Taba (1933 – present)

Master Taba was born July 5, 1933, in the Tomari district of Naha City. Master Taba bagan his study of karate at the Nagamine dojo when he was 15 years old. Master Taba selected the Nagamine dojo because he respected Grandmaster Nagamine's reputation and the reputation of his dojo. Master Taba has trained his entire life under the tutelage of Grandmaster Nagamine. Master Taba, like many of the other Matsubayashi-ryu senior instructors, has begun his own organization. The All Okinawan Shorin-ryu Karate Association is intended to perpetuate Nagamine's rich heritage.

Master Taba

Master Taba's favorite kata is Wankan. Master Taba possessess a stocky build and is very poweful, and he feels that Wankan is ideally suited for someone of his body structure. His favorite weapon is the nunchaku.

Master Taba is perhaps best recognized in Okinawa for his devastating punching power, which he largely attributes to years of diligent training on the makiwara. The reason Master Taba places such emphasis on makiwara training is because he believes developing the proper punching technique is the primary resource of karatemen. Proper punching technique, according to Master Taba, can only be achieved with proper hip technique. Makiwara study is one of the few ways to develop hip technique.

Chapter 1 — Lineage

Master Taba adheres to the philosophy that a strong defense is a practitioner's best offense. Taba explains that if an opponent attacks your face, the karate practitioner can kill the attack by punching the opponent's punch. In other words, blocking techniques are also effective offensively.

Master Taba and Sensei Ota

2
Sensei Eihachi Ota

It was in Naha city, the capital of Okinawa, at the age of 12, that Ota began his study of martial arts. After gaining recognition as one of the strongest in his high school's karate club, Ota was invited to join Grandmaster Nagamine's private dojo. However, when growing up, Ota trained mostly at Master Shima's dojo because it was closer to his home. As a youth, Ota enjoyed playing baseball and boxing in nearby gymnasiums. Yet, his passion for martial arts was evident even at such an early age, and karate ultimately consumed all of his time.

Today, Sensei Ota vividly remembers his training in Okinawa under Grandmaster Nagamine and his senior disciples Chokei Kishaba, Kensai Taba and Masao Shima. Master Kishaba was always revered as one of the toughest fighters in the karate world. Sensei Ota recalls that Kishaba often visited the Shima dojo and conducted special classes. Master Kishaba ran a private dojo in Naha City but only the strongest minded of karate students were allowed to join.

Master Kishaba's brother is one of highest ranking Goju-ryu adepts and the Grandmaster of the Yamane-ryu kobudo lineage. Many senior students amuse at how the parents were forced to separate the youths, requiring them to attend different karate schools and study different styles to avoid any boy-

Sensei Ota

hood rivalry. Today the brothers are respected as two of the strongest karate men, particularly for their practical applications of techniques in combat situations. Sensei Ota points out that men like Kishaba trained for "life-and-death" situations. This, Ota propounds, requires a different level of physical and mental commitment. Sensei Ota quietly explains to his students that the modern day emphasis on point fighting is very different from the way students traditionally trained in Okinawa, even up to the time that Ota was training at the Shima dojo.

Sensei Ota, in his typically soft spoken and quiet demeanor, sometimes reminisces about his training in Okinawa. He remembers when he realized that training in Master Shima's dojo was not enough. He likens this to academic pursuits as well. A student should attend classes, Ota asserts, to acquire knowledge, but must do homework and continually exercise outside the regular classes to hone and retain that knowledge. In this way, martial arts is no different. Contemporaries of Ota in Master Shima's dojo remember the story of how very late one evening a senior instructor went to Ota's parents' home because Ota had refused his promotion to first-degree black belt. The senior instructor was sure Ota would be home because it was so late in the evening. Instead, he found Ota practicing karate in a nearby school yard training alone and in complete darkness. This was the first time anyone at the dojo found out about Ota's supplementary training.

Chapter 2 — Sensei Ota

Once his secret was discovered, Sensei Ota has to explain that he did not intend any lack of respect to his contemporaries or seniors at the dojo. Rather it was his desire to achieve a higher potential that drove him to train more than other practitioners. Sensei Ota explains that the wonderful thing about karate is that it is impossible to fully reach a state of perfection. That is, training is a process, an evolution of knowledge and technique in which the practitioner can continually keep improving. As soon as one goal is accomplished, there is immediately a harder one that the practitioner must strive to achieve. Sensei Ota tells his students that complacency, or the belief that you have maximized your potential or ability, is the first step in your downfall.

Receiving instruction from Master Shima

Sensei Ota constantly reminds his students of the importance of striving for more. According to Sensei Ota, getting to black belt level is relatively simple. However, most people stop there, even in Okinawa. Very few students continue to develop their skills, let alone improve enough to move to the next level. Students of Ota's attest that his speed and skill continues to improve over time, despite growing older, and that is what differentiates him from ordinary athletes. Whenever people complain that they are too old, Ota reminds them that Grandmaster Nagamine trained daily until his death at 90 years of age.

Sensei Ota encourages students to make karate a way of life. The dojo in Okinawa is open 24 hours a day, 7 days a week, even

Receiving instruction from Kishaba

during holidays. When Ota left Okinawa to pursue an electronics degree at Tokyo University, he was forced to work during the days to pay for tuition and devote evenings to study. He did not have time to join a dojo, but it did not deter him from practicing karate. His five-foot by seven-foot apartment in Tokyo became his new dojo. It is said that he would practice so hard that other residents thought there was an earthquake. Practitioners who know Ota tease that it is probably safer to be in an earthquake than to have to face him in a sparring match.

In 1969, Sensei Ota moved to the United States. Despite being thousands of miles from his homeland, he always kept training. His students recall that Sensei Ota has never missed a day of training, even following a severe motorcycle accident in which he was seriously injured. When his students found out about the accident, they were shocked. They didn't even know he had been injured. It was impossible to tell from watching him train. Often Sensei Ota tells injured students, "If you hurt your right side, then use it as an opportunity to train with your left and build up your weaknesses. Always make yourself stronger by working on your weaknesses."

In 1973, Ota opened his first dojo in the United States. Still, he always remembers the training as substantially more serious in Okinawa. Classes in Okinawa would continue to the point that sometimes students would see blood in their urine when they went to the bathroom after class. The difficult part, however, according to Ota, wasn't the pain, but building up the fortitude to go and do the same thing again the following day.

Sensei Ota married in 1980. His wife owned a sake bar for 15 years in one of the roughest areas of Los Angeles. It was such a tough neighborhood, police officers were known to exclaim

Kishaba with sai

that the only time they felt safe in the "hood" was in Sensei Ota's bar. One neighborhood police officer, who later became a student at the dojo, recounts a story of how three hardened criminals, armed with firearms, attempted one evening to rob the sake bar. Their attempt failed. Several gun shots were fired, but, even with their firearms, the three assailants just were not fast enough to handle the lightning speed of Ota's techniques.

Sensei Ota is also an expert in many of the traditional Okinawan weapons. Sensei Ota believes that kobudo, the study of weapons, is an integral part of karate training, and he encourages students to practice with the various weapons. Sensei Ota says that weapons training presents an opportunity for students from different styles to train together because the techniques needed for weapons are the same, regardless of stylistic variations or a practitioner's background. Always, however, the student must first learn how to take care of the weapons. In this way, students develop respect and appreciation for the weapons, and, moreover, the responsibility and control to wield them.

Perhaps even more than his lightning speed or the forcefulness of his techniques, what differentiates Sensei Ota from all other sensei is his mastery of "distance." Ota explains that when opponents engage, they are already at a very short distance from one another. But, in a fight it is critical to learn to control the long distance situations before engaging an opponent. Students must work on their combinations to achieve a higher level of skill. Once Ota was challenged to a life-and-death fight by a champion full-contact kick boxer from Japan. Yet, after watching Sensei Ota execute several combinations while warming up before the duel, the Japanese fighter bowed out of the contest, thinking it better to lose face than to risk his life.

Sensei Ota explains that students who concentrate on techniques for short distances may indeed develop deadly blocks and punches, but can easily be defeated because they have not developed a strategy to cope with combinations, fakes, feints and shifting movements. Many senior students are quickly overwhelmed by Sensei Ota once they encounter his lightning-fast combinations, shifting stances and foot movements. Sensei Ota is frequently invited to Okinawa to conduct sparring courses because of his mastery of these strategies.

Okinawan karate and kobudo were passed on for centuries from teacher to student, in private and by word of mouth. It has only been in the past couple of generations that teachers have set their thoughts and philosophies down in written form. The primary impetus for contributing to this work rests on Sensei Ota's belief that in this modern age, practitioners learn from other mediums like books, videos and the Internet. Teachers must adapt to the changing environment or their teachings may not survive the way they did through generations in Okinawa. Learning can be enhanced by a book or video. Moreover, those materials that are currently available on the market can be dramatically improved. It is Sensei Ota's sincere hope that this work is a step in the right direction.

Section Two
KATA

3
Kata

Grandmaster Nagamine's book, *The Essence of Okinawan Karate-do*, is widely considered to be the definitive text on Matsubayashi-ryu. The kata section of that book includes an extensive photographic record of the 18 kata in the Matsubayashi Shorin-ryu system. Grandmaster Nagamine himself painstakingly posed for each of the photographs, numbering close to a thousand.

Having compiled the modest work before you, the authors can attest to the fact that producing those photographs was not easy. The process is time consuming and laborious. Why then did Grandmaster Nagamine bother go to all that trouble? What was the intention behind the kata section of his book? The same question could be asked of Shotokan Grandmaster Gichin Funakoshi when he supervised the production of photographs for the kata section in his book titled *Karate-do Kyohan*.

One possibility is that Nagamine and Funakoshi were attempting to catalogue the myriad kata that would document their respective systems of karate for historical purposes. Yet, this cannot be the sole purpose. They could have catalogued the style without taking step-by-step photographs of every kata. In fact, creating a record for future generations could not even have been the primary purpose since neither Nagamine nor

Funakoshi provided verbal explanations of the history, philosophy, applications of movements, or technical explanations for the techniques in their respective treatises, except perhaps in the most general way.

Another possibility is that they were creating a reference guide for the legacy of their respective styles. Certainly, neither Nagamine nor Funakoshi could have imagined that inexperienced practitioners would actually learn kata from a book. Even for the experienced practitioner, learning a new kata from photographs is virtually impossible. It is undeniable, however, that these books are photographic reference guides.

In *Unante: The Secrets of Karate*, John Sells writes, "Kata should be seen as repositories of karate theory as well as the classical definition of each style. In fact, at one time, the word kata was actually synonymous with style."

To a certain extent, Nagamine helps to define Matsubayashi-ryu with a photographic record of his kata. But, any kata by nature evolves over time. Significant kata design changes were introduced and incorporated into the kata by such legendary karate masters like Sokon Matsumura, Anko Itosu and Chotoku Kyan, all extremely important figures in the genealogy of Matsubayashi-ryu. Also, certain kata were undoubtedly taught differently during different periods throughout a master's lifetime. Moreover, some masters, from Matsumura to Nagamine, purposely taught different variations of the same kata to different students.

In a strange but effective way, teaching kata this way forces students to develop greater insight into the depth and levels of understanding practitioners can attain through the study of kata. Sometimes changes may be instituted by the founder of a particular style, but not completely disseminated to all students. This issue is particularly relevant for large worldwide organizations such as Matsubayashi Shorin-ryu and the Japan

Chapter 3 — Kata

Karate Association. Therefore, if Nagamine or Funakoshi really intended their books to be used as reference guides, then they would have to have made a new photographic record every few years to accurately reflect the natural evolutionary process of the kata and their styles.

In Sensei Ota's dojo, students frequently rely on Nagamine's book as a reference tool, but only as a way to learn the sequence of the movements. It does not help practitioners to learn the movements themselves. The difficulty with Nagamine's book is that it does not show the movements in between the poses. In other words, although Nagamine's book shows us the proper position at the beginning and the end of a particular movement, it does not show how to get from one position to the next. Moreover, Nagamine's book lacks any discussion of the techniques themselves, the applications of movements and the philosophy behind the kata. And yet it is those elements more than any others that embody the true essence of the style.

What follows is an attempt to further the practitioner's understanding of the small, yet critical movements that take place between the photographs in Grandmaster Nagamine's book. The authors' intent is to develop a greater appreciation for the history and evolution of the Matsubayashi Shorin-ryu kata, as well as a valuable resource for learning techniques. Sensei Ota urges practitioners to use this book as a necessary supplement to *The Essence of Okinawan Karate-do*, not as a substitute. Sensei Ota feels strongly that they are meant to be read together as compliments to one another.

It would be impossible to give technical explanations for every move in each kata; therefore, Sensei Ota has tried to identify the most salient parts of each form or the movements that cause the most misunderstanding or confusion. Naturally, these explanations are Sensei Ota's interpretations of the kata and may differ from other practitioners' interpretations. Nevertheless, it is his goal to provide explanations that best capture the essence of the defensive themes or karate theory which are preserved in the kata.

INTERNAL TIMING VERSUS EXTERNAL TIMING

The primary objective of kata practice is to develop what Sensei Ota refers to as "internal" timing. Internal timing refers to the coordination of the movements of the entire body in perfect synchronization to generate maximum power at the moment of impact. Achieving proper internal timing requires perfect coordination of every moving joint and muscle in the body, with special focus upon the flex of the knees and ankles, the rotation of the hips and shoulders, and the snap of the fist. When all these elements are timed correctly and combined with proper breathing, the practitioner will be able to deliver blows with a power that far exceeds their size and weight.

To Sensei Ota, this ability to generate power far beyond the practitioner's size and weight is one of the most unique and remarkable aspects of karate. The practitioner's success ultimately depends upon the proper execution of his technique, and not upon size or weight. That is appealing to Sensei Ota because it means that no person is at an advantage, merely because of his innate physical characteristics.

When practicing kumite, nothing is certain and the practitioner must be ready for all types of attacks, fakes, feints and combinations. The distance between combatants constantly changes and the practitioner must learn to continually adjust. By learning to adjust to constantly changing circumstances, the practitioner develops what Sensei Ota refers to as "external" timing.

Unlike kumite, in kata practice, there are no surprises. The practitioner is faced by several imaginary opponents who attack from different directions. Yet, kata is done the same way each time. There are never any surprises. The practitioner always knows which direction to face and in what order the imaginary opponents will attack. The objective in kata training is to turn as quickly as possible to face and engage each new oncoming attacker and then execute the proper counterattack. Each movement should demonstrate the proper balance, speed and power. Through constant repetition of these pre-arranged movements, the practitioner learns the proper body mechanics that enable him to develop the proper "internal" timing.

Many karate practitioners do not devote enough time to kata practice to develop "internal" timing. Instead, they move too quickly to kumite practice. For tournament competition, this type of training is adequate because point-fighting techniques do not have to be effective in real life situations; the practitioner only has to exhibit superior "external" timing.

Sensei Ota is not trying to discount the importance of tournament training. He is merely observing that for street situations the karate practitioner must also possess internal timing as well as external timing. Otherwise, their techniques might not work against powerful or experienced attackers. Conversely, possessing internal timing without external timing is not effective for the street either. Practitioners that only practice kata and not kumite often get defeated in street situations because they are only trained to react to imaginary, pre-arranged situations.

KATA BODY MECHANICS

To have proper body mechanics, the practitioner's body must function like a "spring." To uncoil, a spring must first be squeezed tightly together. When a spring is compressed, it cre-

Okinawan Karate

ates tension which stores potential energy. This tension or energy is potential because it is ready and waiting to be released. The amount of tension determines the subsequent speed and power with which the spring will uncoil when it is released. The more tightly the spring is compressed, the more tension is created and the faster and more powerfully it will uncoil. In karate, the practitioner trains his body to function like a spring, so that one can create tension and store energy that is released when executing karate techniques, particularly combination movements.

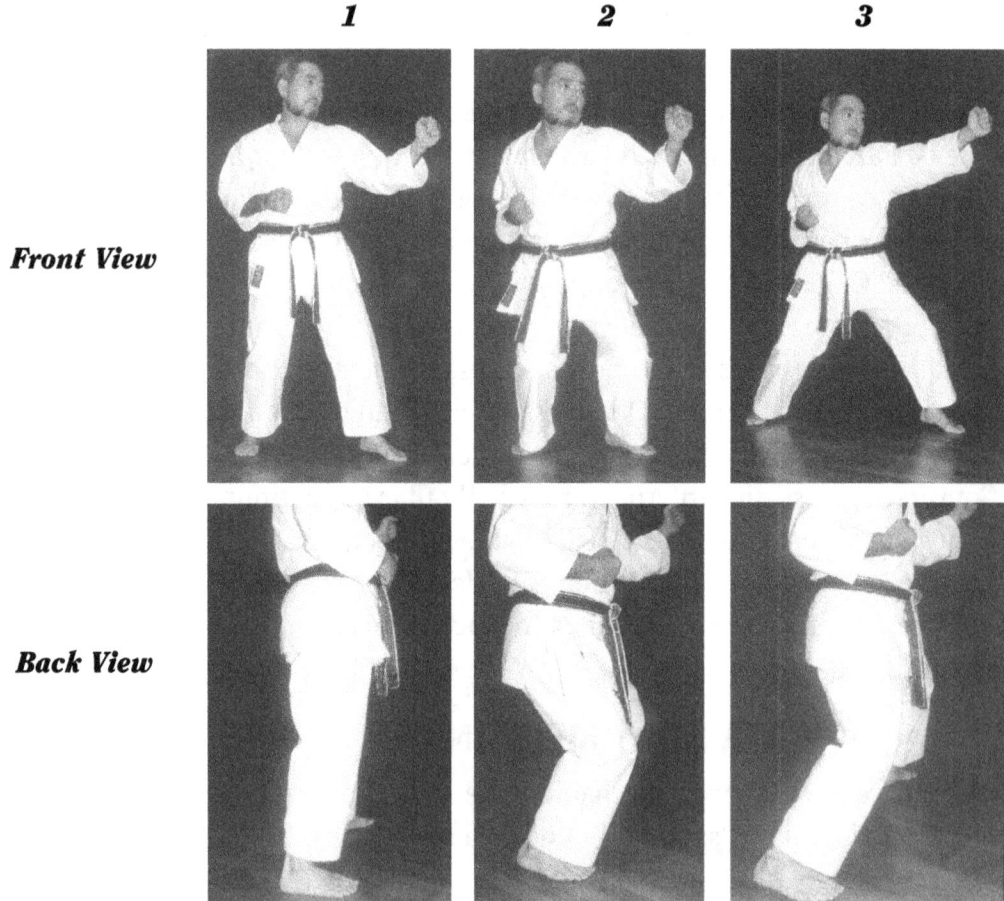

Front View

Back View

In karate, closing the distance from an opponent is a fundamental and critical skill to master. The speed and efficiency at which the distance to an opponent is closed can determine the outcome of a fight. According to Sensei Ota, kata training develops the ability to "squeeze the spring," thereby creating tension and storing energy. That energy is released when the practitioner "uncoils the spring." The more tightly the practitioner is able to squeeze his body tightly together like a spring, the more power he can generate upon delivery.

Dropping the Weight

Lowering the body's center of gravity helps the practitioner to become more grounded and thereby enhances his ability to generate power for striking or punching. Shorin-ryu blocking techniques are generally executed in the cat stance position. However, punching techniques and counterattacks are generally executed in the back stance position, which is essentially the same as the cat stance except with a lower center of gravity. According to Sensei Ota, practitioners need to develop their stances in a way that allows them to quickly drop their weight from a blocking stance (cat stance) to a counterattack stance (back stance) in order to generate power on the striking technique. This is done by bending the rear leg or supporting leg.

Blocking Stance   *Striking Stance*

Dropping the weight also helps the practitioner to build tension in the legs and joints. When the spring is compressed tightly together, it creates tension, which in turn generates the subsequent speed with which the spring can uncoil. To change distance from an opponent or to change direction in kata, it is essential to first drop the weight to store up the energy, just like a compressed spring.

Controlling the Joints

Coiling up the body tightly to create tension depends upon the practitioner's ability to control the muscles and tendons surrounding the joints in their bodies. Certain joints are especially critical: the toes, ankles, knees and hips.

In Shorin-ryu karate, power is generated by releasing that tightly coiled tension all at once in a concentrated explosion of energy. The movements of all the joints in the body must work in unison. Many Shorin-ryu adepts assert that the most distinctive feature of their style is that power is derived from a snapping, whip-like action, and not from pushing or forcing the techniques. Snap comes from twisting the body and hips forward, and then quickly retracting them backward and with precise coordination. The more control a practitioner has over his joints, the more snap will develop, and consequently the more power he will be able to deliver with his techniques.

Controlling the joints is what enables a practitioner to shift in and out to change distance between himself and his opponents. It also determines how well the practitioner can shift from one stance to another to change the space between himself and his opponents. Shifting from a back stance or cat stance to a forward stance and vice-versa, changes the space between the practitioner and the opponent. The way a practitioner manipulates space and distance, especially in close or confined areas, can determine the outcome of a fight.

The practitioner's control over his joints determines not only the speed at which the spring can uncoil, but also the ability to control the forward momentum. In order to recoil the spring, or to shift backwards to evade an attack, the practitioner must have enough control over his joints to stop his movement suddenly. Control of the joints is what distinguishes the snapping type of techniques in Shorin-ryu from the pushing type of techniques used in other styles.

Whip-like Techniques

It is particularly important for striking techniques — like kicks and punches — that the practitioner's body function like a whip, with the hips acting as the fulcrum. To achieve this whip-like action, the practitioner must keep his muscles relaxed and use the hips to bring the body back. As with a whip, it is the pull back or snap on the punches and kicks that creates the power, not the extension alone. The snap is achieved by pulling back or retracting the strike instantly at the moment of impact. The snap is controlled by pulling the arm and hand back with the proper timing. Sensei Ota refers to the proper extension and pulling of the techniques as "internal timing."

Changing Direction

Changing direction and turning are imperative skills for self-defense, especially when facing multiple attackers. When changing direction in kata, the lead leg determines the direction or angle of the turn, and it also determines the distance from the opponent. The rear leg generates the speed and power. Remember to drop the weight to create tension before turning or changing angles, then spring into the next position by using the rear leg and joints to uncoil the spring.

Changing direction requires mental focus and concentration. In kata, it is important to come to a complete stop both physically and mentally before beginning a new sequence of moves or engaging a new opponent. Developing the mental discipline to be able to stop suddenly and then quickly move again

in another direction is especially important when facing multiple attackers.

Stepping Back Into the Cat Stance

Moving away from an attack and landing in the cat stance is a quintessential skill for karate practitioners. Indeed, it is the primary skill developed in the Pinan forms. When landing in the cat or back stance, the practitioner must learn to put tension on the rear leg by having the weight already dropped the moment when the rear foot touches the ground.

When stepping back, practitioners will often only move their rear leg. It is critical, however, to move the entire body and to keep the weight over the rear leg. When stepping back or sideways at an angle to avoid an attack in a back or cat stance, it is critical to move the entire body, and not merely the leg. Keep the body over the rear leg and land with it already bent at the knee and the weight already fully dropped. Landing with the weight already down in a back or cat stance helps to increase the tension in the joints. This increases the subsequent power of the next technique, which most likely is a counterattack. In addition to increasing the power of the next technique, landing with the weight already dropped eliminates taking more time later to squeeze the spring to store the energy in the joints.

Posture

The back should remain erect in all stances at all times. The upper body should remain relaxed, while using the legs to determine distance, direction and height.

Incorrect

Correct

Do not bend at the waist, especially when moving from one position to another, changing directions or turning. Bending at the waist or leaning forward compromises the practitioner's balance and makes it difficult to move efficiently. When sliding in and out to adjust the distance from an opponent, leaning forward and bending at the waist requires substantially more time and effort for the practitioner to respond to an attack, especially if the attack comes from side angles. The practitioner must first regain balance before he can turn to face an attack from a side angle. A delay in the response time could easily be the difference between success and failure in a self-defense situation.

In all stances, it is important to make sure that the upper body and shoulders are not square to the front, facing the opponent. The upper body should be angled at 45 degrees to the opponent. This is fundamental for two reasons. First, if the body is too square, it exposes the "center line" to attack. In contrast, when the shoulders and body are turned 45 degrees, the body is easier to protect. Second, when the shoulders are square to the front, the hips are already fully rotated, so there is no built up tension to release.

Okinawan Karate

Notice how Sensei Ota creates tension in the wrist joint by twisting his hand the opposite direction of the blocking motion. This generates maximum snapping power.

The spring must be squeezed by pulling the hip and shoulder back to where the upper body is at a 45-degree angle away from the opponent. Then it is cocked and ready to uncoil with an attack. Moreover, the weight must be on the rear leg to push off. If the body is square, it is difficult to focus the weight on the rear leg.

Blocking

In Shorin-ryu karate, as with striking, the most important part of the blocking technique is the snap. When blocking, the snap is primarily a function of wrist control. As soon as contact is made, the wrist should snap quickly and strongly enough to deflect the angle of the opponent's strike. If contact with the

Chapter 3 — Kata

When executing a mid-level block, the arm — from the hand to the elbow — should remain at the same level throughout the technique. This protects the vulnerable areas of the body against attack.

opponent's attack is made at the proper distance from the practitioner's own body, then even a small deflection in the angle of the opponent's attack will result in significant changes by the time the blow reaches its maximum extension.

Once a practitioner has developed proficient snapping technique with his blocks, he will not have to move his arms very far to deflect incoming strikes. At that point, even in actual self-defense situations, the practitioner only has to use his blocks to defend a small, limited area directly in front of his body. Furthermore, with proper snap, practitioners can develop blocking techniques that release such devastating power that the blocks themselves become effective as offensive moves as well, even generating enough force to break an opponent's bone. In this way, blocks and strikes can serve a similar purpose.

Note that in Shorin-ryu karate, the blocking hand should always be on the outside when crossing the arms in preparation for a blocking technique.

SPEED AND TEMPO

Kata, and especially the advanced kata, lends itself to personal interpretation. This is ultimately what makes karate an art and not a science. According to Sensei Ota, however, practitioners should experiment to gain a better understanding just as scientists design experiments to test their hypotheses. In theory, once a theorem is proven, all contrary theories are abandoned. Yet, in martial arts, truth is not necessarily universal; it is highly individualized. That is, the best method for one practitioner may not be the best method for another.

One area that is often debated is the proper speed at which a given kata should be performed. Should the speed and tempo of a given kata be open to individual interpretation and the anatomical make up of the practitioner?

Sensei Ota tries to approach this issue in a logical manner. Sensei Ota acknowledges that the fundamentals (discussed in the body mechanics section of this chapter) must always be executed properly. Admittedly, some practitioners have longer legs, arms, etc., which may require more or less time to move from one position to another. The correct speed and tempo, therefore, is when those movements are executed at maximum speed without compromising the internal timing of the techniques. We have already established that internal timing is the ability to use the different parts of the body in unison to generate maximum power.

It is important that practitioners do not rush or hurry because in doing so they sacrifice the proper execution of their techniques. According to Sensei Ota, the best way to increase speed in kata is achieved by accelerating the time between movements. In other words, by speeding up the "set-up" time or preparatory steps that are required to move into the next position. This is particularly true when the practitioner is required to turn or change direction. Minimizing the set-up time is critical to increasing speed.

Decreasing set-up time is largely a matter of mental discipline, not of physical ability. To Sensei Ota, this is why kata practice is an essential part of the mental discipline of karate. When a practitioner is tired, the first area which breaks down in kata performance is mental focus. The set-up period generally breaks down first and the result is the entire kata is executed too slowly. The hardest thing for practitioners to do is to maintain their focus and not lose concentration throughout the duration of the kata, especially when preparing for the next movement. This is why Sensei Ota has made such an extensive effort to photograph each of the movements between the steps for all of the 18 Matsubayashi-ryu kata which follow.

FORCE vs. POWER

At a recent gathering where several martial arts practitioners were in attendance, a heated discussion ensued between fighters from various disciplines and styles. One person argued that the amount of power an individual can generate is entirely a function of weight and muscle mass. His position was that a 200-pound fighter would always be able to generate more power than a competitor who weighs 150 pounds. Therefore, he contended, weight categories are essential in fighting competitions. All the wrestlers and grapplers who were present, as well as all the boxers, completely supported this view.

Ironically, Sensei Ota was at the table where the discussion occurred. It made the authors wonder what Sensei Ota thought about the subject, especially since he was the only man in the room weighing less than 150 pounds! Later when he was kidded about the conversation, all he did was smile.

Before offering a counter argument, first let us examine the argument made by the other fighters. They contended that, assuming that the fighters were of equal technical ability, power was purely a matter of weight and muscle mass. In scientific terms, their argument can be expressed by the following equation, which is familiar to any student of physics:

$$\textbf{Force = Mass} \times \textbf{Acceleration}$$

According to that argument, a fighter's mass is comprised of his weight and muscle. Yet this scientific formula still has one other variable: acceleration. In order to produce equal force with a smaller mass, the acceleration must increase proportionally. Therefore, even according to their own formula, a fighter of much smaller body mass can theoretically produce the same amount of force as a heavier opponent if his blows are delivered with greater acceleration.

Therefore, if they conclude that smaller men cannot generate equal force, they must assume that smaller men cannot generate sufficient acceleration in their techniques to counter the effects of greater mass. Thus, the only way to achieve fairness in a fighting match is to institute weight rules.

To counter the position the other fighters took, we would suggest that they have never seen techniques delivered with the speed and acceleration of a master like Sensei Ota. If they had, they would never again question the amount of force that can be generated by a person weighing less than 150 pounds.

Moreover, Sensei Ota has always expressed his conviction that force is only important up to a certain point in a fight. The human body can only withstand so much damage. After that, anything greater becomes redundant.

Chapter 3 — Kata

Therefore, if both fighters can generate sufficient force to achieve that threshold, other issues like technique and footwork are the differentiating factors that determine the outcome in a fight. Perhaps that is why, when questioned about the other fighters' argument, Sensei Ota only smiled.

There is no doubt that mass and acceleration can produce sufficient force to meet that threshold, even for a person weighing less than 150 pounds. However, in karate the objective in striking techniques is not merely force, but power. This may sound like a lot of semantic rhetoric, but the difference is critical.

Power is not as easy to define as force. Power involves mass and acceleration, but also something more. Power is a function of snap, both the extension *and* retraction of a strike, and not merely the pushing motion that is defined by the concept of force. Snap requires proper technique and internal timing and demands years of diligent study. In karate, even a small, improvement in technique can mean an exponential difference in the amount of power that is generated by a given technique.

Karate practitioners do not attempt to use striking techniques to penetrate through an opponent's body. To deliver power, as opposed to merely force, once contact is established, the technique is retracted instantly to create a snapping action. Penetration occurs when a practitioner focuses on a target six inches past the point of contact. The only way to penetrate is with force, not power.

Imagine a large pane of glass as a metaphor for the human body. If a practitioner punches the glass, attempting to penetrate using force by focusing on a target six inches beyond the point of contact, the punch may penetrate, but the effect on the human body would only be the equivalent of making a tiny whole, barely larger than the size of his fist. Conversely, if the practitioner strikes the plane of glass but does not extend past and instead recoils immediately upon contact, the equivalent effect on the human body would be like a tiny crack in the glass made by the two lead knuckles. Nevertheless, the resulting effect would cause a concussive wave starting at the point of contact that would shatter the entire glass. That is the difference between force and power.

The application of power versus force has its consequences in combat as well. When a practitioner like a boxer hits his opponents, the opponent falls away from the practitioner. The same is true of any technique that pushes more than snaps. When an opponent falls away, the practitioner must pursue to continue the attack. That allows greater opportunity for the opponent to recover. Conversely, when proper snapping technique is used to generate power, the opponent is drawn closer towards the practitioner, making it easier to execute the ensuing combinations.

This is not to suggest that a karate practitioner who generates power with proper snapping technique will necessarily defeat fighters from other disciplines. Sensei Ota has always said that, in fighting, success is determined by the man and not the style. Nevertheless, the karate fighter, unlike boxers or wrestlers, does not need to rely on weight categories because the outcome depends more on power than on force.

The kata covered in this text are as follows:

> Fukyukata I
> Fukyukata II
> Pinan I – V
> Naihanchi I – III
> Ananku
> Wankan
> Rohai

Chapter 3 — Kata

Wanshu
Passai
Gojushiho
Chinto
Kusanku

Ostensibly, it would have been impossible to attempt to detail every movement in each kata. Rather, an attempt was made to focus and discuss the most significant movements, as well as the movements which are most commonly misunderstood.

On our two research sabbaticals to Okinawa, we discovered that senior Okinawan instructors often had added extensive details in the margins of their copies of Grandmaster Nagamine's book, *The Essence of Okinawan Karate-do*. We have intentionally left room between the pictures so that students have room to write in their own personal remarks and notations. We feel this is an important part of the learning process.

4
Fukyukata I

Fukyukata I was composed by Grandmaster Shoshin Nagamine, the founder of Matsubayashi-ryu. Nagamine thought that the Pinan kata were too difficult for beginners, so he added Fukyukata I and II to his system of karate. Fukyukata I develops eye focus and mental concentration. Because of the basic rhythm and nature of the movements, Fukyukata I lends itself to practicing together in a large group by doing the kata according to a single count for each movement. Unlike advanced forms, the rhythm and tempo of this form remains the same throughout the kata. Each time the practitioner turns or changes direction in the kata, he should mentally come to a complete stop, then move as quickly as possible to the next direction to confront the next imaginary opponent. Sharpening these mental skills considerably enhances reflexes and physical speed during the execution of techniques.

Fukyukata I also develops the practitioner's ability to move from a high stance or natural stance to a low stance or forward stance and vice-versa. This is critical to the beginner's understanding of distance. Karate techniques are optimized at specific distances. If too close to the opponent, punches and kicks can be jammed or blocked. If you are too far away, strikes lose power or fail to reach the target. Achieving the proper distance is a skill which requires constant practice. The front leg determines both the direction or angle the practitioner faces and the distance from the opponent. The rear leg determines the speed and power of the practitioner's technique.

Fukyukata I also develops the practitioner's ability to change direction and angles. To build this skill, the practitioner must learn to drop his weight in the stance, concentrating all the tension on the rear leg. Then the practitioner must use this tension to push off in the new direction toward the opponent. The feeling in these movements should be like squeezing a spring tightly together and then releasing the energy all at once.

#2. *When moving from the ready position to a forward stance facing to the left, it is critical to spring into the forward stance with as much speed and snap as possible. Before springing into the forward stance, it is important to first drop your weight. Keep the hips torqued.*

#4. *Students frequently lose their balance when practicing at full speed. In order to learn to control the body and come to a complete stop, focus on the left knee. To generate speed from the ready posture, focus the energy upon the large toe and the second and third toes of the right foot. Use these to push off and accelerate. As soon as the left toes touch the ground, they must grab the floor firmly to make a stable base. Without the ability to control the feet, it is impossible to snap the hips and generate enough force to stop an*

Chapter 4 — Fukyukata I

attacker. The hips must be ready to begin twisting the moment the left toes touch the ground. These principles also hold true whenever the practitioner changes directions such as in: **7, 11, 20, 24, 28, 32, 38** and **42**.

5 6 7 8

#5–6. When changing from a low stance like the forward stance to a higher stance like the natural stance, it is important to change height gradually. Step forward with the knees bent. Moreover, keep the hips and the shoulder pulled back when stepping forward. This builds the tension in the body. When punching, stand up while twisting the hips and turning the body. Many students incorrectly stand up before they step in to punch in the natural stance. This telegraphs the movement and allows the opponent to move away before the practitioner can deliver the counterattack. This fundamental holds for: **9–10, 13–14, 22–23, 30–31, 40–41** and **44–45**.

9 10 11 12

#17. *Notice how his entire body is torqued for maximum spring-like explosion.*

#18. *There is considerable debate over the best way to make this turn and subsequent change of direction 135 degrees counter-clockwise. Sensei Ota contends it is better to start by moving the right foot on the heel as far as possible.*

#19. *Then the toes grip the floor as quickly as possible.*

#20. *Push from the toes through the knee and follow the connection through the hips to the shoulders. The other way to execute the turn is to rotate on the ball of the right foot until the heel comes around 135 degrees. The difference is the time it takes to make the turn and change direction. Sensei Ota believes his method is better because it saves considerable time and, moreover, it makes it far easier to generate speed and power. Additionally, in combat it is very difficult to fend off an attacker at close distances when moving the heel out and turning around to block.*

Chapter 4 — Fukyukata I

#24–27. *When executing the rising block in this kata and in all subsequent kata, do not raise the elbow. Rather, imagine punching straight upwards at something above the head.*

Okinawan Karate

Chapter 4 — Fukyukata I

37   38   39   40   41

42   43   44   45   46

65

5
Fukyukata II

Fukyukata II was composed by Chojin Miyagi, the founder of Goju-ryu. Both Fukyukata I and II were created with the purpose of teaching karate-do to school children in Okinawa. The governor of Okinawa prefecture selected Grandmaster Nagamine and Grandmaster Miyagi for this important assignment, and both kata were created for this purpose in 1940. In the Goju-ryu system, the form is referred to as Gekisai I. Grandmaster Nagamine included Miyagi's kata in his curriculum as a beginning level form.

1   2   3   4   5

#2. *As soon as the right toes touch the ground, the practitioner should push from the toes through the knee and hips to generate power on the rising block.*

6 7 8 9

#6. *This movement can be executed several ways. Whatever the method that is used, it is critical to protect the ribs when sliding backwards into a horse stance. Some practitioners protect their ribs with the opposite hand that punches. Then the arm moves over and the hips coil to prepare for the block. Sensei Ota, however, protects the ribs with the same hand that delivers the high punch. The hand drops to cover the ribs, as the opposite arm crosses over to prepare for the block. As soon as the practitioner drops into the horse stance, the arm and hips are cocked and ready to snap. This method of executing the movement is preferred because the practitioner can protect the rib cage and at the same time make early preparation to block. This elimination of an extra move is more effective for street situations. This is consistent with **14**.*

Whenever stepping back to avoid an attack, the practitioner must set up to block at the same time or he will not be in a position to execute the blocking technique, especially against a formidable opponent. Perhaps in kata, distance and timing are secondary, but in kumite they are everything.

Chapter 5 — Fukyukata II

10   11   12   13

#10–12. When executing the rising block, the practitioner should not raise the elbow. Rather, imagine punching straight upwards with a upper cut motion to a target at just above head level.

14   15   16   17

18   19   20   21

69

Okinawan Karate

#24. *Sensei Ota recommends that practitioners practice this sequence by shifting the weight onto the rear leg for the block and then shifting it back to the front for the punch. To develop maximum power, practitioners must learn to use their hips. The rear leg controls hip rotation, which makes it necessary to transfer the weight onto the rear leg to coil the spring. When performing the kata, this transfer of weight is not emphasized. Nevertheless, Sensei Ota's method is preferable for practice because it helps build speed and power. This also holds for* **35.**

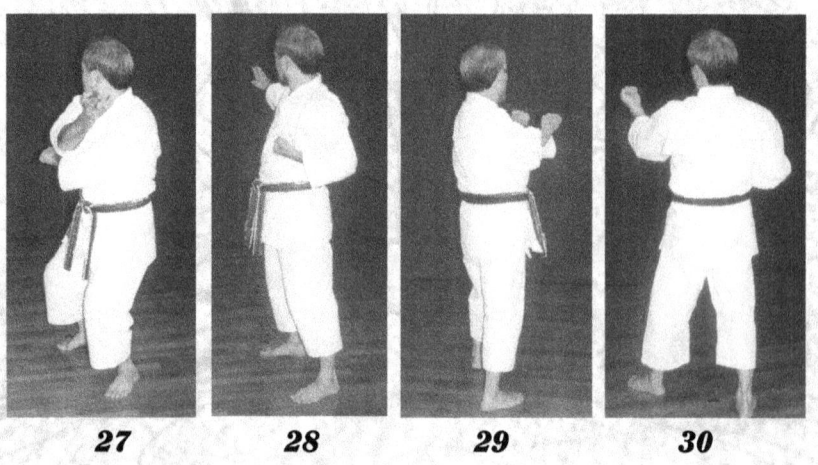

Chapter 5 — Fukyukata II

#27. *When standing up, cross the arms to prepare for the blocking movement. Notice that the blocking hand is facing up to create additional snap on the block. Crossing the arms in this fashion accomplishes two important things. First, the left hand is guarding the ribs, which otherwise would be exposed. Second, by crossing the arms, the practitioner generates more power on the block because of the push-pull tension created with the arms. The same principle also holds for **38**.*

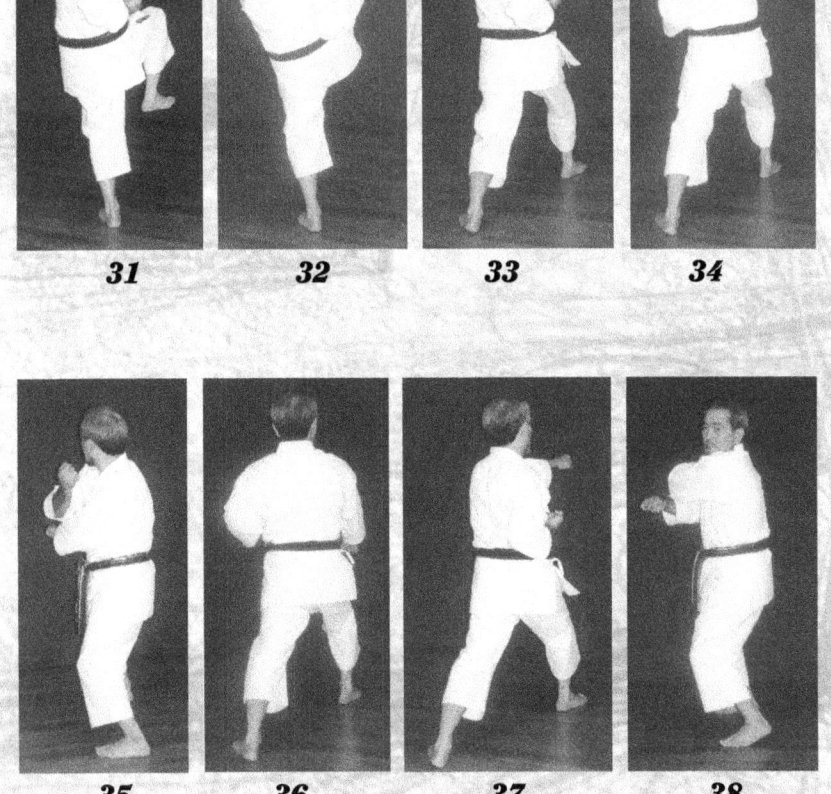

31   *32*   *33*   *34*

35   *36*   *37*   *38*

71

Okinawan Karate

39 *40* *41* *42*

43 *44* *45* *46*

Chapter 5 — Fukyukata II

6
Pinan Kata

Most historians believe that the Pinan kata were composed and introduced after 1902 by Anko Itosu (1813–1915), the legendary karate master from Shuri. Others, however, contend that Itosu only created Pinan V, and the other four forms existed before his time. To support this argument, Chosin Chibana (1885–1969), the founder of Kobayashi-ryu and one of Itosu's top students who is known for faithfully passing on Itosu's teachings, only taught Pinan V in his later years out of respect for Itosu. Itosu was one of the most accomplished students of Soken Matsumura, and a teacher to Chotoku Kyan and Choki Motobu, two of Grandmaster Nagamine's most prominent instructors. Pinan kata has many techniques and sequences that are similar to the Matsubayashi-ryu version of the Kusanku kata. Therefore, many believe Itosu derived Pinan from this form. Others, like John Sells in *Unante: The Secrets of Karate*, argue that Itosu modeled the Pinan kata after the "Channon" kata taught by Matsumura. Very little is known of these Channon forms, and others, like Patrick McCarthy, have suggested that it is also possible that the Channon kata was the same form as Kusanku.

When karate was first introduced publicly in the high schools in Okinawa, Itosu did not want to give the impression that karate-do was about violence or aggression. Consequently, he intoduced Pinan kata. Translated into English, Pinan means "peaceful mind." Pinan kata are useful for helping to develop a mental state in the practitioner that is like a Zen state of awareness. That is, the mind is relaxed and yet completely alert at the same time.

In Pinan kata, the practitioner is surrounded on all sides by several imaginary opponents, but he does not know from which direction the first attack will come. Developing a peaceful mind is critical. Otherwise, the practitioner will be unable to react to an attack by multiple opponents. It is essential to learn to clear the mind of all distractions to change direction fast enough to prepare for the next attack. On the street, especially when adrenaline can make it difficult to maintain a peaceful mind, it is necessary to concentrate on one opponent at a time, then prepare to face the next as quickly as possible without hesitation.

All five Pinan kata begin with an imaginary opponent attacking from the left. In Matsubayashi-ryu, it was decided that on the first move of each Pinan kata the practitioner should move away from the attack by stepping back with the right foot and twisting into a cat stance. In other Shorin-ryu styles, the practitioner moves into the oncoming attack by moving the left foot first. Psychologically, this is an enormous difference. Sensei Ota feels the way this technique is performed changes the entire nature and philosophy of the Pinan forms.

According to Sensei Ota, Pinan kata is about developing the skill to move out of the way of harm by stepping at an angle in the cat stance. The practitioner must land with the weight down so that the spring is already tightly compressed once the practitioner's leg touches the ground. In Pinan, the practitioner learns to move away from the opponent's attack, which is a fundamental skill, especially for beginner- and intermediate-level practitioners. In more advanced kata, the practitioner develops the skill to move in when being attacked. The first time in the Matsubayashi-ryu curriculum that this technique is used is in the opening move of Wankan kata.

In Pinan, step at an angle, away from the attacker, which puts the practitioner at an advantageous position to deliver the counterattack. As soon as the toes of the right foot touch the ground, use the legs to snap the hips and generate power on the blocks. When the practitioner steps back to avoid the attack, he must land with his weight already dropped, so that the coil is already compressed. This enables the practitioner to generate greater speed and power on the subsequent counterattack.

Before turning or changing direction in Pinan, or any kata, the practitioner must always look in the direction of the attack. This may seem simple or even obvious, but Sensei Ota has learned that it is one of the most common errors made.

The Reinforced Block

Some practitioners place one fist on the elbow when executing this maneuver. This provides extra support on the blocking arm; hence the name "reinforced" block. To Sensei Ota, this interpretation is counter to the way blocks are executed in Matsubayashi-ryu. That is, all blocking techniques are performed with snap to deflect the incoming attack. The moment the practitioner's arm makes contact with the opponent's body, the arm and hand immediately snap to generate power. Placing the other hand on the elbow does not generate extra snap or power. At most, it may provide support for a type of pulling or pushing block, which may be consistent with other styles, but not Shorin-ryu. In Shorin-ryu karate, the stylist deflects the blow by snapping the wrist upon contact with the opponent's arm. Shorin-ryu practitioners do not pull or push with the arms.

Sensei Ota's preferred interpretation is that the other arm is guarding the ribs against a potential kick, while the blocking arm is defending against a punch. This is exactly the same premise behind the hand positions on the shuto. Sensei Ota believes this is also the proper way to execute a reinforced block. The arms should snap in the same way that they do when executing a shuto.

Chapter 6 — Pinan Kata

I. Pinan Shodan

Okinawan Karate

#2. When stepping out into the cat stance, the body should already be twisted with the spring coiled and the weight dropped. This holds throughout the entire Pinan series of kata.

#4. It is important to twist the upper body on the inside block. This builds up body tension and sets up the counter punch on the subsequent punch with the reverse hand. The weight must be low, concentrated in the legs to control the upper body. This principle also applies to 8 and is the same body mechanics as the movements in Passai kata (see **Passai 8–11, 12–15, 17–20** and **21–24**).

#5. On the counter punch, it is important to drop the weight from a cat stance into a back stance. At the same time the practitioner drops his weight, he should initiate the punching movement. When dropping the weight, bend the back knee. This drops the entire body into a back stance. Many students make the mistake of only dropping the heel of the front foot in the cat stance, and this does not lower the center of gravity. This is a key to perfecting this technique because "grounding" the body by dropping the weight helps to generate power on the counter punch.

Chapter 6 — Pinan Kata

6   7   8   9   10

#10. It is important to stay low when the rear leg steps up for the block. Maintain a consistent height.

11   12   13   14   15

#12–13. Keep the supporting leg bent on the front snap kick. By keeping the supporting leg bent, it is possible for the practitioner to control the distance from the opponent.

#14. When the right leg front snap kick returns, place the right foot on the floor in the correct position to make the turn. Drop the weight as the foot lands on the floor to build up the tension in the body. The body should already be twisted when the practitioner turns around. The left arm must be held tightly against the body.

Okinawan Karate

16   17   18   19   20

#16. *When stepping in to execute the shuto, turn the shoulders. The bottom hand that guards the ribs comes up to the shoulder to prepare for the next move. Keep the bottom arm tight against the body the entire time. This holds for everytime the practitioner moves forward to execute the shuto.*

#20. *When stepping in to execute the spear-hand strike, stay low and keep the hip back. This is exactly the same fundamental skill developed in Fukyukata I when the practitioner steps forward to punch.*

21   22   23   24   25

Chapter 6 — Pinan Kata

26 *27* *28* *29* *30*

31 *32* *33* *34* *35*

#31. *The right arm, which is protecting the ribs, should come directly up to the left shoulder to begin the subsequent block. Keep the arm tightly against the body and twist the body and shoulders.*

#32. *Keep the right knee behind the left. Both legs must mutually support each other, and the knees must be tight. If the weight distribution is off, then the practitioner will not be able to execute the snap kick smoothly on the counterattack.*

Okinawan Karate

36 37 38 39 40

41 42 43 44 45

Chapter 6 — Pinan Kata

46 *47* *48* *49*

50 *51* *52* *53*

85

Okinawan Karate

Chapter 6 — Pinan Kata

II. Pinan Nidan

Okinawan Karate

Chapter 6 — Pinan Kata

Okinawan Karate

26 27 28 29 30

31 32 33 34 35

#34–35. *When executing this sequence of lower shuto in the cat stance, it is critical to bend the knees deeply and to bring the weight down when moving from cat stance to cat stance. This lowering of the center of gravity is what creates power and stability on the technique. Learning to bring the weight down while maintaining balance in the stance is, according to Sensei Ota, an extremely important skill for kumite.*

Chapter 6— Pinan Kata

36 37 38 39

#36–37. *Sensei Ota is pictured with the correct form on the lower shuto. Notice the arm is slightly bent and the wrist is straight. When executing the lower shuto, it is important that the wrist snaps in order to deliver the power necessary to block an opponent's attack. The snapping motion is the same on the lower shuto as it is for the mid-level shuto in Pinan I and other kata.*

40 41 42 43 44

91

Chapter 6 — Pinan Kata

III. Pinan Sandan

93

Okinawan Karate

#3–7: *Simultaneous blocking drill. Sensei Ota sees this sequence of moves as a coordination exercise for the body, not as training for fighting or self-defense. Sensei Ota argues that this sequence is not intended to be a fighting technique because the simultaneous blocks are executed in a standing position or natural stance, instead of the lower stance that is typically used when blocking. This is not to insinuate that these exercises are not important training because they are. But, these kinds of techniques do not have much practical application. In kata, not every move has to have a practical fighting application. Some moves are valuable specifically as training exercises to condition the body.*

Chapter 6 — Pinan Kata

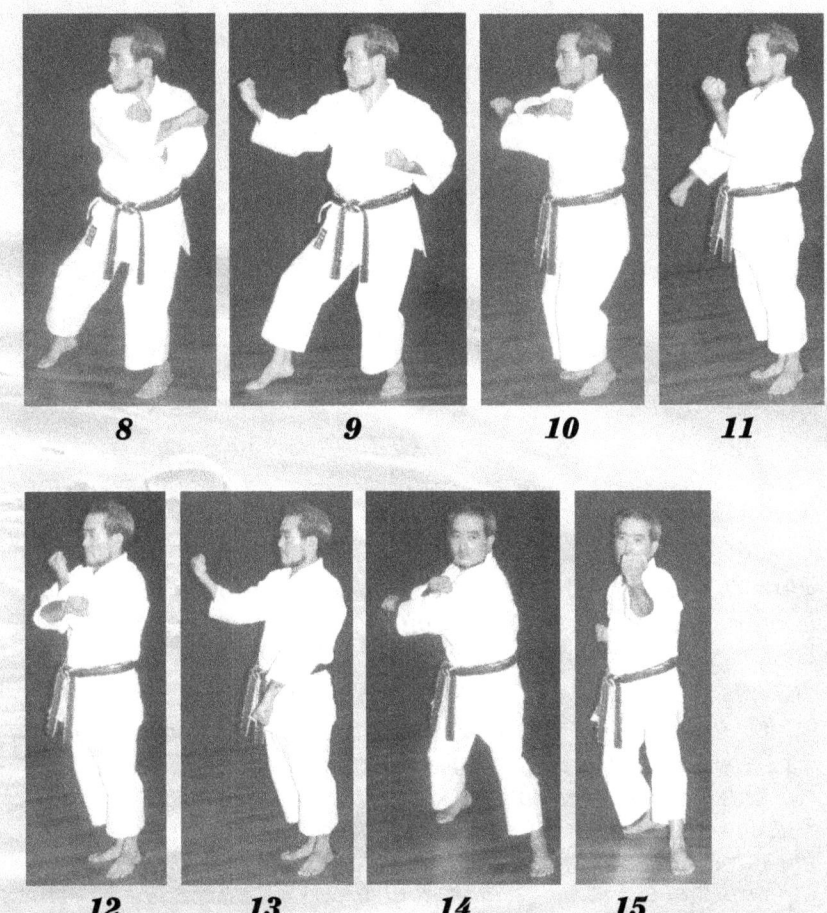

Okinawan Karate

16　　17　　18　　19　　20　　21

#18. *When turning around, it is important to drop the weight. This makes it easier to turn efficiently and to maintain balance.*

#20. *The upper body must twist to build up tension in the body. It is not necessary to punch hard on this move because the other hand is pulling the opponent closer to the practitioner, which increases the power of the technique considerably, like a head-to-head collision.*

#21. *Sensei Ota believes that this technique is really not a punch, but rather is just to establish distance from the opponent. Therefore, it does not need to be that powerful. It is the punch on the subsequent movement that needs to be powerful. Sensei Ota explains that the idea of establishing distance with the first punch is an integral part of other Shorin-ryu forms as well (see Pinan V below).*

Chapter 6 — Pinan Kata

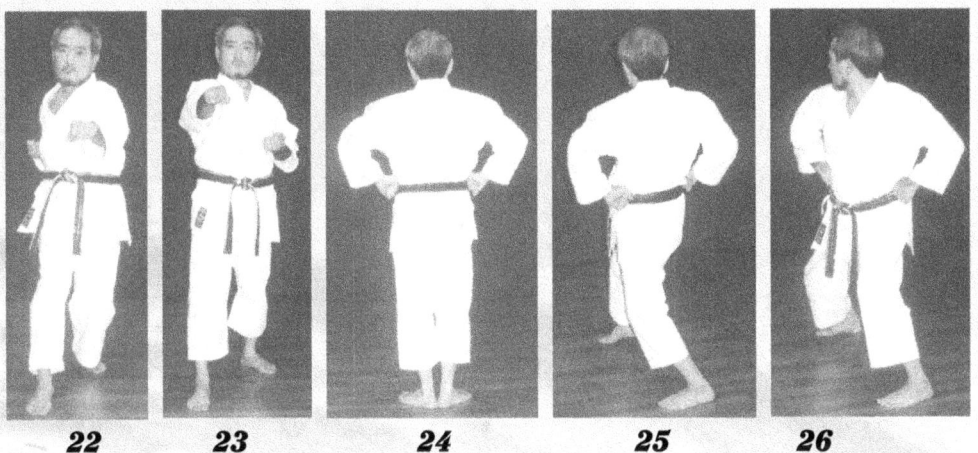

22 23 24 25 26

#24. *By standing with the arms on the hips, the practitioner is inviting the imaginary opponent to attack.*

#25–26. *Again, this series of three elbow blocks is largely for training and exercise and is not practical for fighting. But the purpose is to build tension in the body and derive power from the hips. The block is not made by moving the shoulder, but by rotating the hips.*

27 28 29 30

#27–30. *Following the elbow block in the sequence is a backfist to the opponent's face. Do not start the backfist from the hip. Rather bring the arm into position, then execute the counterattack. When examining the bunkai, it becomes clear that if the practitioner attempts to deliver the backfist from the hips, it is impossible to hit the opponent in the face because the opponent's body will block the trajectory of the practitioner's attack.*

97

Okinawan Karate

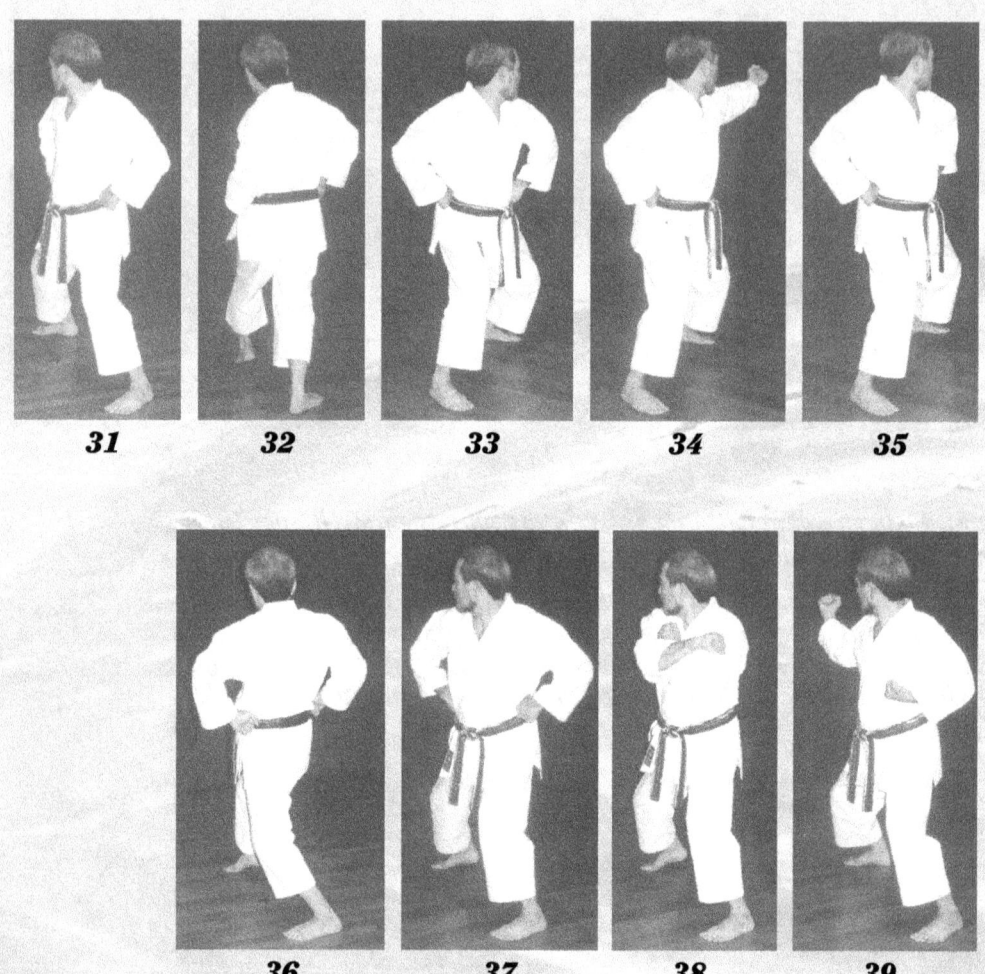

Chapter 6 — Pinan Kata

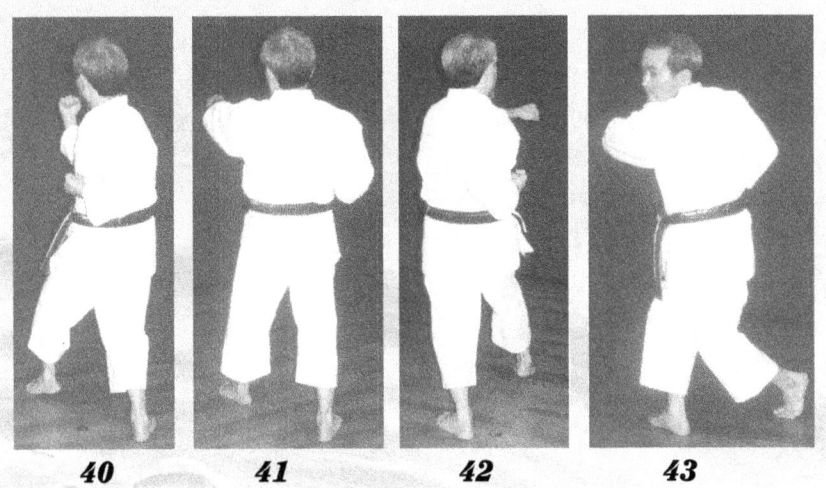

#42–43. When turning around, it is critical to drop the weight, just like 18.

Chapter 6 — Pinan Kata

IV. Pinan Yondan

Okinawan Karate

#6–7. *Keep the arms close to the body when twisting. The right arm is punching.*

Chapter 6 — Pinan Kata

#11–12. *The purpose of the kick is to establish distance from the opponent in order to deliver the elbow strike.*

#20. When the left leg steps out, the practitioner must coil the spring to create the tension in the body. This is done by twisting the body.

#21. The right leg then slides in for the open-hand block. The weight distribution must be correct to maintain balance.

#25–26. Lift the right foot and pivot on the ball of the left foot.

#27. When the practitioner lands, the weight must be on the back leg. If not, then the practitioner has to transfer the weight to the rear leg before punching. This dramatically delays the delivery of the counterattack.

Chapter 6 — Pinan Kata

29 *30* *31*

#29–30. When executing the front kick, keep the supporting leg bent the entire time and the height consistent. Keep the right shoulder back when kicking. This makes the kick quicker and avoids telegraphing the kick, which is critical for kumite.

#31. When the practitioner lands back in the back stance to execute the double punch, the weight should already be fully dropped the instant the foot lands on the floor.

32 *33* *34* *35*

105

Okinawan Karate

36 37 38

39 40 41 42

Chapter 6 — Pinan Kata

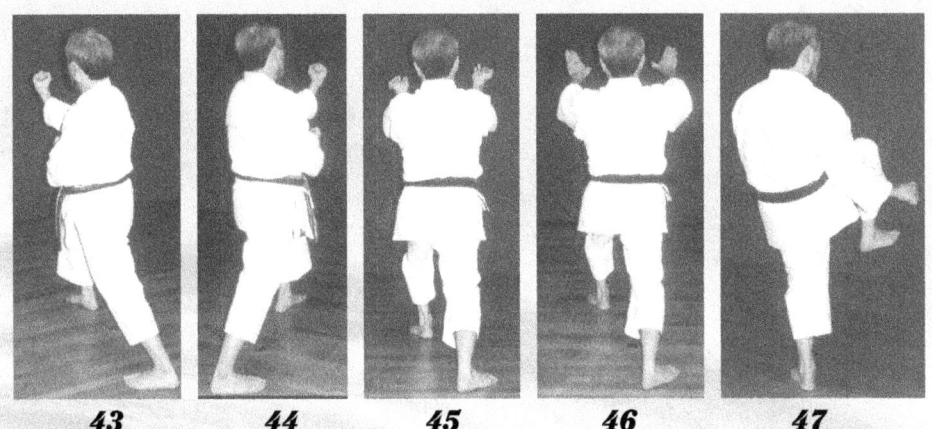

#45–46. *The right arm reaches to the opponent to grab and pull him over.*

107

Chapter 6 — Pinan Kata

V. Pinan Godan

Okinawan Karate

#4. *On the reverse punch, drop into the back stance, thus lowering the center of gravity. This adds power to the punch by increasing the body tension. The weight is dropped by bending the knee of the supporting leg.*

Chapter 6 — Pinan Kata

13   14   15   16   17   18

#15–16. When shifting backwards from a forward stance into a cat stance, maintain the same height. When the practitioner brings the arms back, he must keep the arms tight against the body. When the practitioner executes the double-arm block, the left arm moves like a shuto.

#18. This arm is establishing distance, like a push. It is not punching. The powerful punch is the ensuing technique. When establishing the distance, drop the body weight.

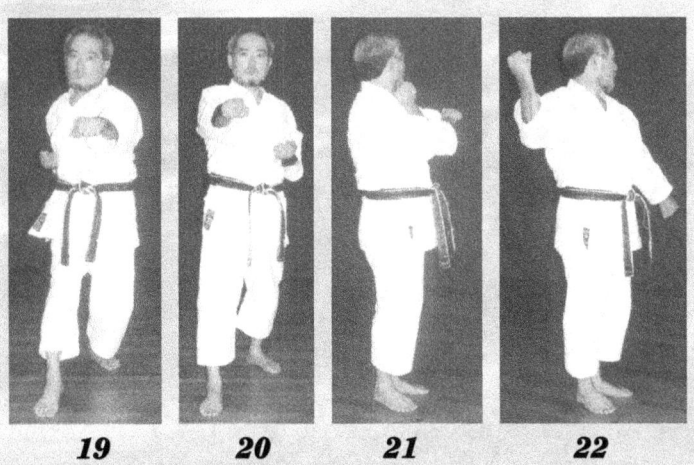

19   20   21   22

Okinawan Karate

#23–24. Drop the weight before moving into the horse stance. Executing this move in any other way can potentially cause the loss of body control and balance. The arms must cross to prepare for the block. Keep the blocking arm tight against the body.

#26–27. This move is performed immediately following the lower block in the preceding move. Push off the right leg to get the power on the subsequent block. By pushing off and controlling the joints in the legs, the practitioner derives power from the hips.

Chapter 6 — Pinan Kata

#34–37. *Maintain a consistent height on these moves. Note that the angle of the arms must be parallel.*

7
Naihanchi Kata

The composer of this kata is unknown, but it has long been treasured by karatemen from Shuri and Tomari. Many traditions assert that Soken Matsumura created Naihanchi or based his version on older forms known to him. Most Shorin-ryu styles practice three distinct short forms of Naihanchi. The creation of the last form, Naihanchi sandan, is attributed to Anko Itosu. In other kata genealogies, both Naihanchi nidan and sandan are attributed to Itosu.

Before the creation of Pinan kata in 1907, Naihanchi kata were the first forms taught to beginning-level practitioners. According to Grandmaster Nagamine, the most important purpose of Naihanchi lie not in the fighting skills they develop, but in training the lower parts of the body through slow and steady sideways movements. Developing strong legs and hips are indispensable to karate training. According to Grandmaster Nagamine, the posture for Naihanchi is similar to the sitting posture for Zen meditation, with strength concentrated in the abdomen. Nagamine recalls that the Naihanchi kata were a favorite of Choki Motobu. Naihanchi kata does have practical application for fighting in cramped or closely confined spaces. The punching and blocking motions are short because space is very restricted. To Sensei Ota, the short techniques make

Naihanchi very difficult to master. In this respect, it is useful to think of Naihanchi as technically advanced forms.

Naihanchi, or "Tekki" in Japanese, translated into English means "horse riding stance." This refers to the way the legs are held open to straddle a horse when riding. Some practitioners perform Naihanchi with the knees directed inwards. This, according to Sensei Ota, is an incorrect posture. Some practitioners use this stance because they have not properly developed their legs. Furthermore, in *The Essence of Okinawan Karate-do*, Nagamine does not even mention this stance because it is not a stance that is used anywhere in Shorin-ryu.

When performing each of the Naihanchi kata, once the practitioner drops into the horse stance, it is critical to keep the height consistent throughout the entire kata. The practitioner's height should not fluctuate up and down. According to Sensei Ota, the only way to build power in Naihanchi kata is to increase the body tension by keeping the weight low in the horse stance.

The horse stance is not a strong stance for defense from the front or rear directions. However, it is extremely strong from the left and right sides. The weight distribution is equally spread between the two legs. If the weight is ever transferred to one leg, the practitioner loses all lateral strength in the stance and is therefore vulnerable to attack from both sides. When stepping over to move in the horse stance in a sideways direction, the practitioner must try and shorten the time the weight distribution is over the supporting leg. This is one of the primary skills developed in the three Naihanchi forms.

Chapter 7 — Naihanchi Kata

I. Naihanchi Shodan

Okinawan Karate

#2. *The practitioner should briefly pause and look at the opponent. This psychologically holds the opponent at bay.*

Chapter 7 — Naihanchi Kata

10 11 12 13

#10–13. The first step of this sequence is performed slowly and deliberately with the hand pointed at the opponent. This psychologically intimates to the opponent that the practitioner is prepared for any attack. When the toes of the stepping foot are planted, there is a slight pause, then the eyes shift to the front to change direction. Finish the sideward step, accelerating the speed while the arm holds off the opponent to the side. Then execute the outside block to the front.

14 15 16 17

#18. *When avoiding leg sweeps or low kicks, make sure the weight stays over the center line as the leg is lifted. The horse stance is designed for fighting opponents either on the left or right sides — not from the front or back. The weight distribution must be equally spread between both feet. When a solid base is established in the horse stance, it is almost impossible to push someone over from the side. When weight is distributed unequally over one leg or another, the practitioner is vulnerable.*

#24. *Drop the weight on this block. This also holds true for* **46**.

Chapter 7 — Naihanchi Kata

Chapter 7 — Naihanchi Kata

II. Naihanchi Nidan

Okinawan Karate

1 2 3 4 5

#2–3. *Drop the weight when performing this movement, as with* **10–11**.

6 7 8 9 10

Chapter 7 — Naihanchi Kata

Okinawan Karate

25 26 27 28 29
30 31 32 33
34 35 36 37

Chapter 7 — Naihanchi Kata

Chapter 7 — Naihanchi Kata

III. Naihanchi Sandan

Okinawan Karate

Chapter 7 — Naihanchi Kata

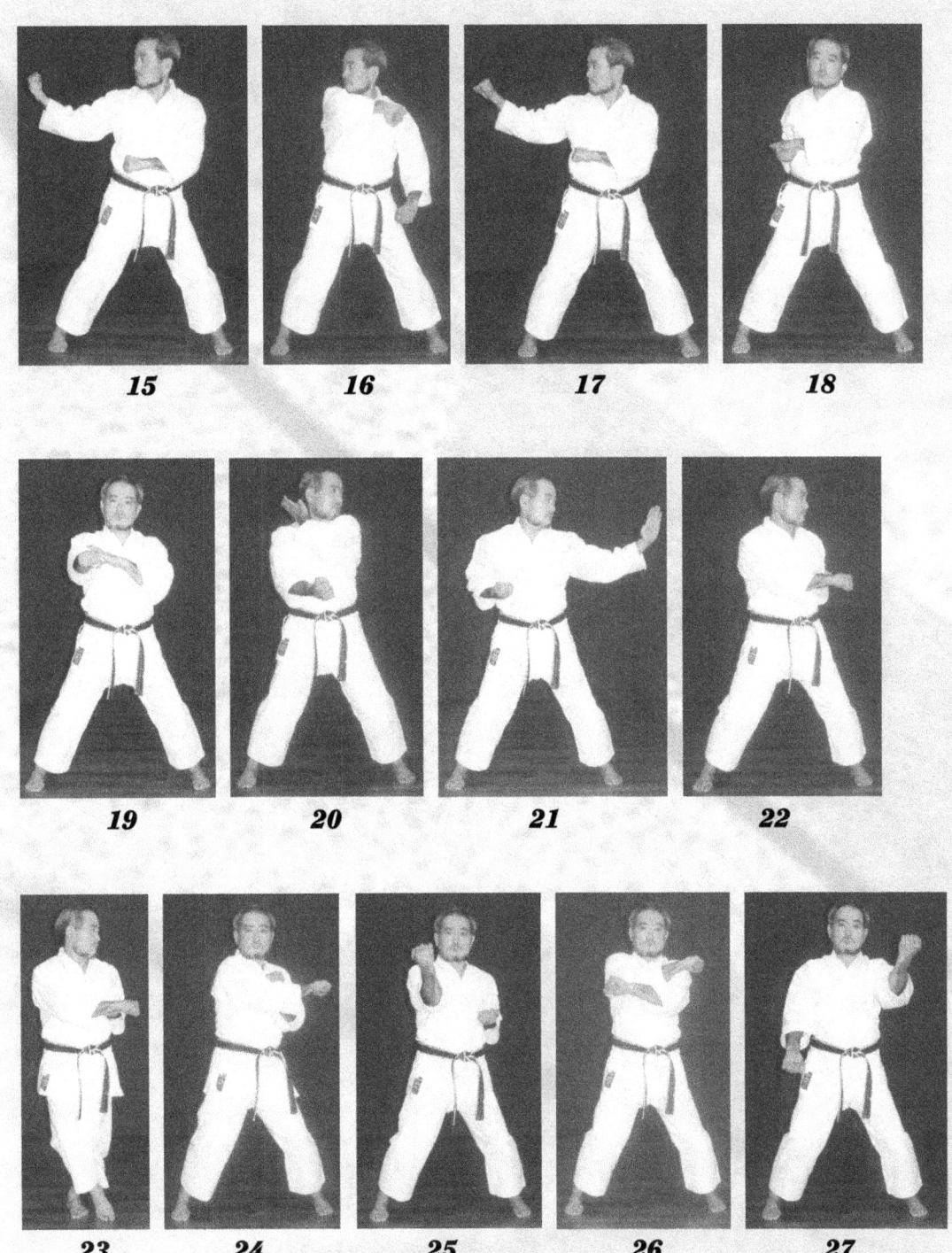

131

Okinawan Karate

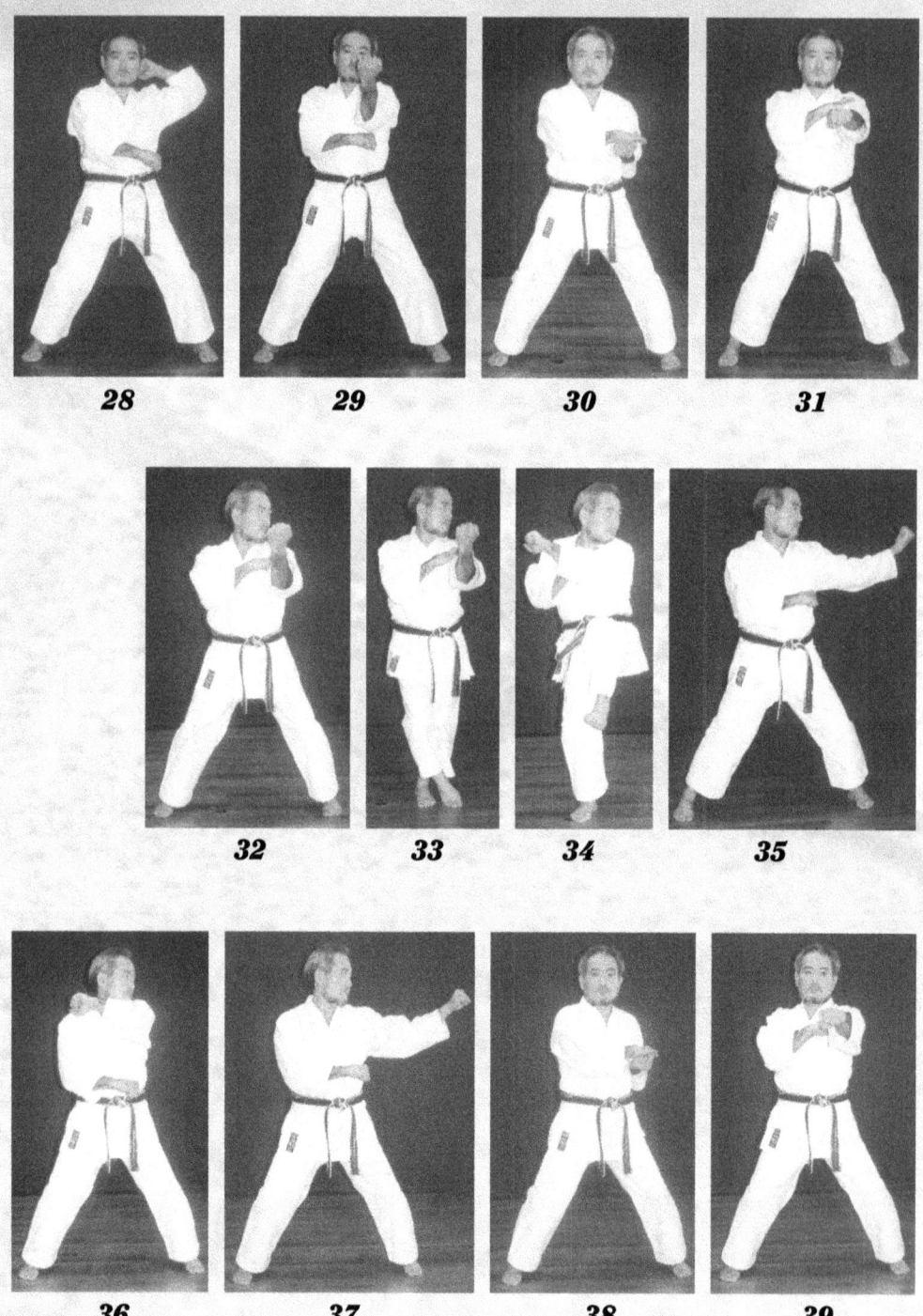

Chapter 7 — Naihanchi Kata

40   41   42

43   44   45   46

47   48   49   50

133

8
Ananku

The composer of Ananku is unknown, and the history is comparatively short. Chotoku Kyan either learned the kata from a Taiwanese who visited Okinawa, or Kyan brought it back with him following a journey to Taiwan. The term "ko" or "ku" means elder, and Patrick McCarthy has suggested that this form may refer to an elder or teacher of Kyan named Anan. It is interesting that practitioners from different schools can practice the same kata, and even claim the same origination of the form, yet the movements and performance may be virtually unrecognizable to each other. We know Ananku genealogically comes down to us through Chotoku Kyan. However, the Matsubayashi-ryu version is unique compared to other versions with the same name.

Ananku is distinguished by its emphasis on the development of offensive and defensive skills in the forward stance. Ananku is the only kata in the Matsubayashi-ryu curriculum in which the practitioner moves backwards to block in the forward stance.

Another important skill practitioners develop by practicing Ananku is the ability to move forward in a front stance while maintaining a consistent height throughout. If the practitioner's height changes, speed is severely compromised. Moreover, the practitioner becomes vulnerable to attack from

Okinawan Karate

the opponent. Practitioners of other styles of karate, particularly the Japanese styles like Shotokan, learn this skill early on in the kata curriculum. In Okinawan Shorin-ryu styles, however, variations of the natural stance are used far more commonly. Therefore, practitioners of Shorin-ryu styles tend to learn to move forward in the natural stance and from a natural stance to a front stance and vice-versa. In Matsubayashi-ryu, developing movement in a front stance comes after learning kata like Fukyukata, Pinan and Naihanchi. Sensei Ota thinks that learning this way of moving is good training and learnming to cover greater distance is a very useful skill, but it does not have as much relevance for self-defense.

1   2   3   4   5

#2–3. *The arms and right foot move together simultaneously. The arm finishes the block at the same time the right foot is planted on the ground. Keep the knee bent and drop the weight when executing this movement.*

The opening sequence of movements is used as a threat by the practitioner to create space between himself and the imaginary opponent. This is not an attack or blocking technique; it is but as a psychological or strategic move. It is the same feeling in the beginning movements of the following kata: **Wankan, Rohai, Passai, Chinto** *and* **Kusanku.**

Chapter 8 — Ananku

6   7   8   9   10

#4–10. *This sequence of moves is important from a psychological perspective because the practitioner is moving in and out. This could even be interpreted as faking and inviting the opponent to attack, and then blocking the attack. This becomes important in kumite because it is strategically very important for the practitioner to be able to induce specific reactions from the opponent. For this reason, Ananku might be seen as a more advanced form than the Pinan kata, even though the movements are generally less demanding to perform from a physical standpoint.*

11   12   13   14

#11–12. *This movement is similar to the movements in Chinto kata (see Chinto **3–5**, **16–18** and **92–94**). However, the left arm is held at the same height as the right arm moves around in a circular motion. In Chinto, however, the left arm starts low and finishes*

Okinawan Karate

in the same position as Ananku. The right arm should move around in a circular motion at a slow and deliberate speed. As soon as the right arm comes fully around and touches the left arm, the next move should be executed at full speed. Sensei Ota's interpretation of this movement is "to invite" the opponent to attack. By moving the arm, it gives the appearance to the opponent that the defenses are down and that the practitioner is vulnerable to attack. Hence, the practitioner is inviting the opponent to attack.

15 16 17 18 19

20 21 22 23

Chapter 8 — Ananku

24 25

26 27 28

#26–28. *Turn the left foot at the same time the body weight is positioned over the left leg to execute the outside block. By turning the left foot, the practitioner builds up tension in the left leg to push off for the next move. This will substantially increase speed. This move comes up several times in Wankan kata as well (see* ***Wankan 6–7, 27–28*** *and* ***42–43***).

Okinawan Karate

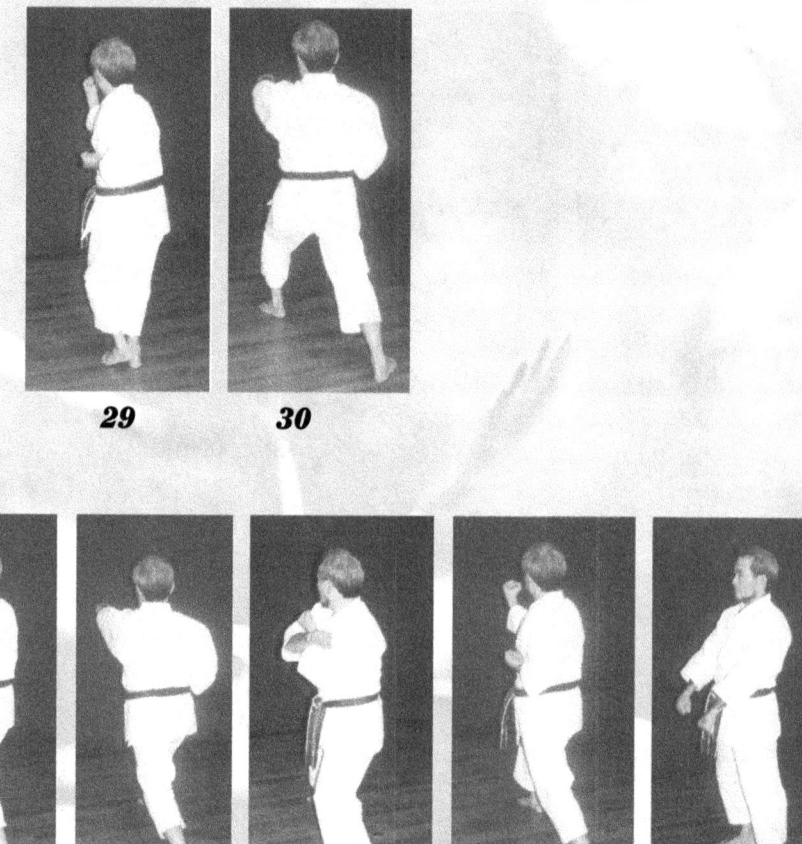

140

Chapter 8 — Ananku

38 *39* *40* *41* *42*

43

9
Wankan

According to Grandmaster Nagamine, Wankan's history is very old. The composer is unknown, but it is one of the few extant kata from the Tomari district of Okinawa. It is important to note that Matsubayashi-ryu is one of the few styles that strives to preserve these Tomari-te traditions. Wankan translated means "the king's crown," but the title does not lend insight into the kata's history or philosophy. The foundations developed in this form are fundamental to learning advanced combinations. Therefore, Wankan is a useful transition from beginning level kata like Pinan and Naihanchi to the advanced level forms like Passai, Chinto and Kusanku. The difference between the combination sequences in Wankan and the higher level forms is that in Wankan the practitioner is not required to move forward or backward when executing the techniques.

Okinawan Karate

#2. Slide in with the front foot. Reach out to cover as much distance as possible.

#4. Slide in with the left foot. Reach out to cover as much distance as possible.

Chapter 9 — Wankan

6   7

#6. *When stepping back into the forward stance, the practitioner is stepping out of the way from an attack coming from a 135-degree angle. The key part of this move is how to build body tension in the hips. This is critical to building the skills to execute combinations with speed and power. The preparation is like coiling a spring. When it is released, the uncoiling creates more speed and snapping of the hips. In order to do this most effectively, when stepping back into the forward stance, keep the right foot angled forward. This maintains the tension in the toes and allows the practitioner to push off from the toes, through the knees, and ultimately through the hips and into the punch. This is consistent with **24** and **38**.*

Okinawan Karate

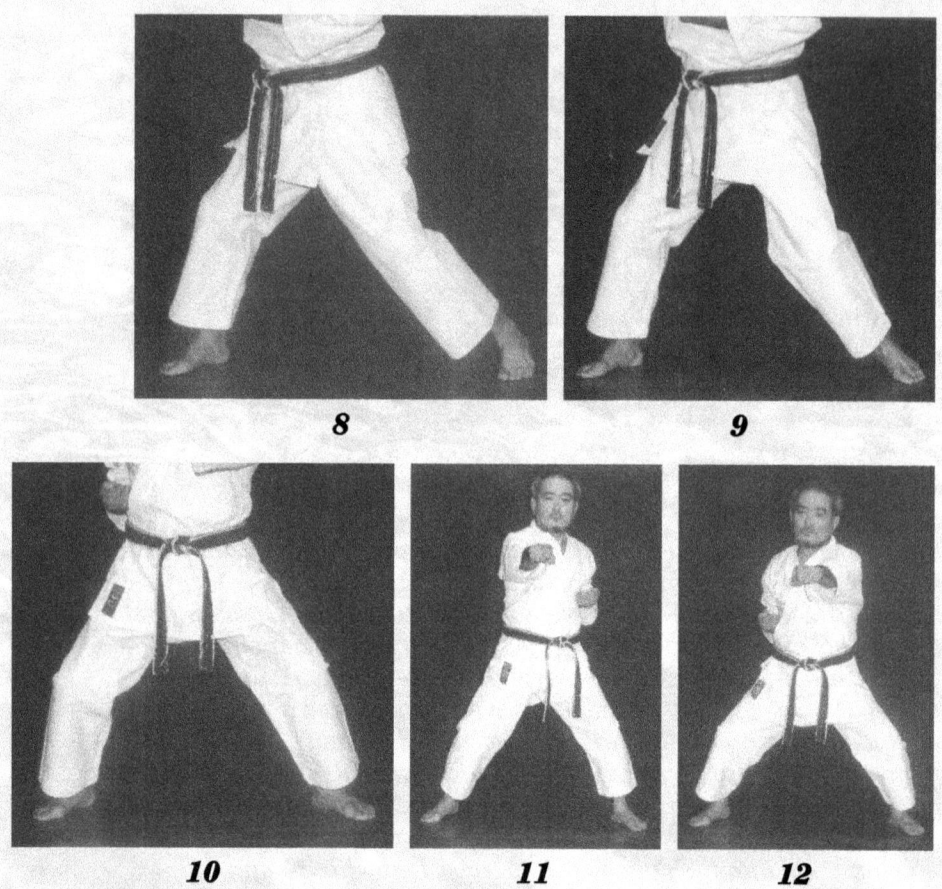

#8–10. *Twist the left foot, thus pulling the left leg in to generate hip power on the ensuing punch. This twisting movement in Wankan teaches the practitioner how to control his hip rotation and how to increase power in his punching techniques.*

Chapter 9 — Wankan

13   14   15   16

#13-14. *When stepping in to execute the double-arm strike to the throat block, the arms are crossed in front of the body.*

#15. *After making the block and before extending the arms to the sides, the arms cross in front of the chest.*

#16. *This move is often cause for confusion. Sensei Ota argues that practically speaking, making a block to both sides of the body against two simultaneous attacks is next to impossible. Rather, Sensei Ota prefers to think of this move as keeping the distance from two potential attackers. By moving the hands to the sides in this fashion, the practitioner psychologically is holding the opponents off on either side by letting them know that he is ready for their potential attack. Naturally, the practitioner does not know from which side the attack will come. Therefore, mental preparedness is essential.*

17   18   19   20

Okinawan Karate

#23. Keep the right arm against the body before making the reinforced outside block.

#25–26. Pull the right arm back to the chambered position. The interpretation or bunkai is that the right arm is pulling the opponent's punching arm down to the side and adjusting the distance with the other hand. The left hand is not really punching; it is pushing or establishing distance from the opponent. Importantly, the heel of the right foot does not touch the ground. The weight is dropped when the right arm punches the opponent. Just like the punching technique in the beginnning of Pinan I following the inside block, the entire body weight must come down, not simply the heel. Dropping the body weight on this punching technique increases the power of the punch substantially.

#27–29. This is like **26** in Ananku. Keep the right foot angled forward. This creates tension in the leg to push off and generate hip power. The left foot controls the hips in order to increase power on the strike.

Chapter 9 — Wankan

30 *31* *32* *33*

#32. *Before sliding in for this short punch, the practitioner should bend his rear leg so he can push off. This is the only way to build power when sliding in for this punch. The same mechanics apply in Wanshu when sliding in to deliver the hidden punch.*

34 *35* *36* *37*

Okinawan Karate

#45–46. *Keep the body weight over the right leg. The left foot changes the direction. Push off the right foot to create power through the hips and move into the lower block. Use the rear leg to push off into the forward stance.*

Chapter 9 — Wankan

47 *48* *49* *50*

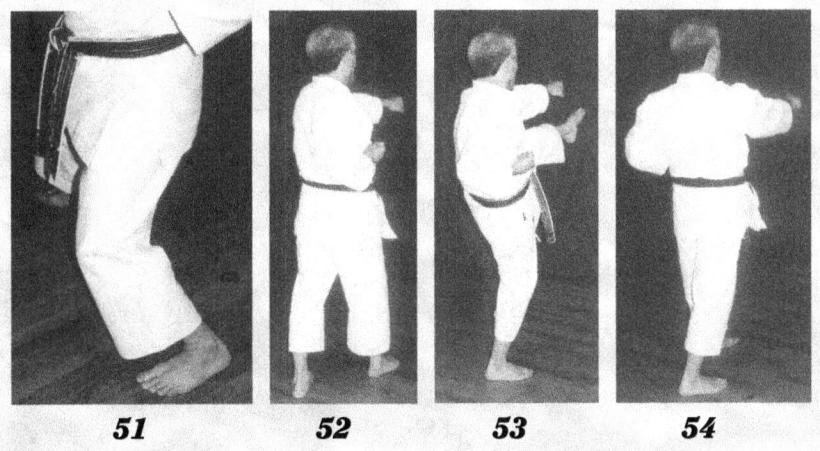

51 *52* *53* *54*

Okinawan Karate

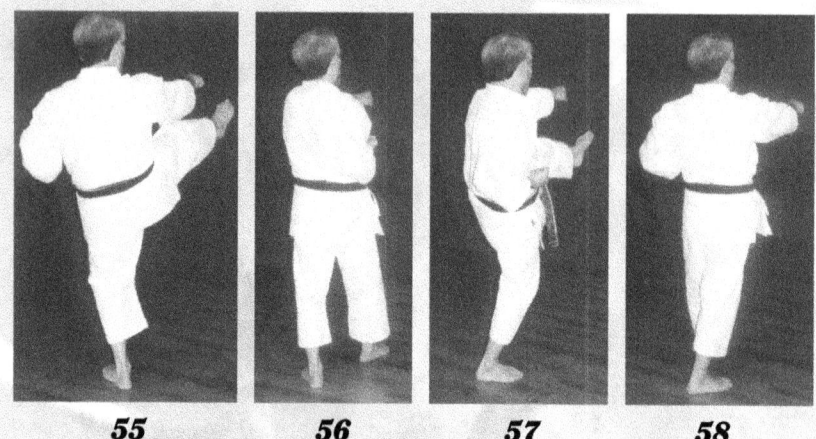

55   *56*   *57*   *58*

59   *60*   *61*

Chapter 9 — Wankan

10
Rohai

Like Wankan kata, Rohai also has a very long history, and also like Wankan, has an unknown composer. More importantly, Rohai is another extant Tomari-te form, passed down through Kosaku Matsumora. Anko Itosu included three versions of Rohai kata in his curriculum, yet most probably they were derived from the Tomari-te form. Translated into English, Rohai means "vision of a white heron." The kata's signature movement of stepping back and blocking on one leg is reminiscent of this title. According to Sensei Ota, Rohai develops continuous rhythm in technique, which is the foundation for quick and powerful combinations. Rohai is the first kata in Matsubayashi-ryu which focuses upon these kinds of advanced combinations and movements, and is therefore a significant leap beyond all the preceding forms.

Master Kishaba

Okinawan Karate

#6–7. *Bring the right arm in tight and twist the wrist. Move the right foot as far as possible to increase the tension in the body. Bring the weight down on the block.*

Chapter 10 — Rohai

9 *10* *11* *12*

#9–10. *The left arm blocks the opponent's arm, then grabs and pulls the opponent forward. The hips provide the power to pull the opponent off balance. Without the hips working together with the grab, it is almost impossible to pull an opponent off balance.*

#11–12. *Drop the body weight on the reverse punch. This is done by bending the knee of the supporting leg. This sequence should be performed as a single count, ending by standing in a ready position with both fists protecting the ribs.*

13 14 15 16 17

#13–15. *This sequence should be performed slowly and deliberately. The practitioner stands between two imaginary opponents who can attack from either side at 45 degree angles. Step forward cautiously with your left foot in case there is a potential sudden attack from one or the other imaginary opponents. Once the practitioner feels comfortable that the opponents are not initiating an attack, the foot is planted firmly. Then the practitioner begins to step forward with the rear leg, still moving slowly and deliberately. As soon as the right toes touch down, the imaginary opponent on the right side attacks. The subsequent movement into the signature Rohai stance should be performed at full speed to evade the attack.*

#16 (The White Heron). *It is critical to step back without losing balance, otherwise the block is ineffective against a real attacker. It is also critical that the practitioner does not lean back when retreating into this stance, otherwise it is increasingly more difficult to move forward to execute the ensuing block.*

#17. *Many practitioners turn the hand flat or parallel with the floor. However, according to Sensei Ota, this will lead to broken fingers or hands. Be sure to keep the hand at the correct angle like a lower shuto, just like the sequence at the end of Pinan II*

Chapter 10 — Rohai

18   *19*   *20*   *21*

#20–21. *Although many Matsubayashi-ryu practitioners execute this movement as a double punch, Sensei Ota feels the first punch is really more of a push to measure the distance. This is why the practitioner remains in a cat stance when executing the technique with the left hand. Then the weight is dropped into a back stance for the punch with the right hand. Dropping into a back stance grounds the practitioner and generates more power on the punch. This sequence of moves is one of the first advanced combinations in Matsubayashi-ryu kata. The sequence begins by retreating into the White Heron stance and executing a simultaneous lower shuto. It finishes with the reverse punch. The practitioner must be able to control his balance when stepping back. The practitioner must also try to move forward and block and then move forward again to establish distance and throw a reverse punch. The sequence begins in an upright one-legged stance, but the practitioner must drop into a lower stance each subsequent step, while controlling his balance. The practitioner should continually build up the speed on each subsequent step during this sequence.*

Okinawan Karate

22 **23**

#22–23. *After mentally coming to a complete stop on the reverse punch, look forward and move the left foot back as quickly as possible. Mentally shift to the front. Shift the body to coil the spring, which will generate power for the punch. The left hand is blocking a kick and the right hand punches the opponent's foot. The twisting and punching mechanics are like* **Wankan 8–10, 28–29** *and* **43–44**.

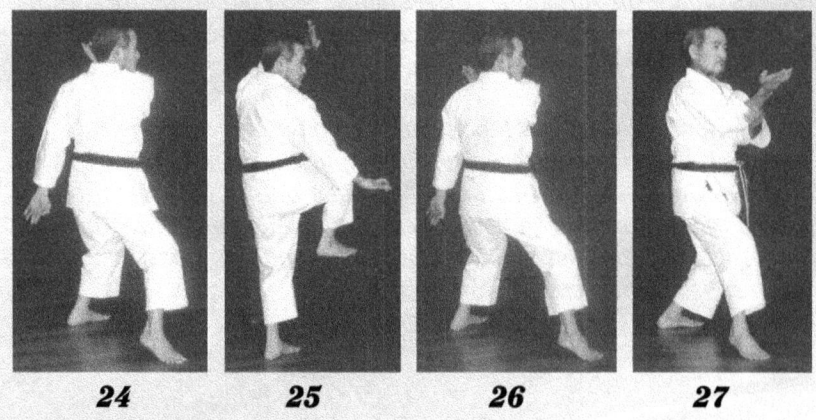

24 **25** **26** **27**

Chapter 10 — Rohai

28   *29*   *30*   *31*

32   *33*   *34*   *35*   *36*   *37*   *38*

Okinawan Karate

39 *40* *41* *42*

#39–41. *This technique is intended for fighting at night or in dim light. The leg moves slowly in an arc, with the foot close to the floor, searching for the opponent. The practitioner should try to cover as much space as possible. It is therefore important to maintain balance over the supporting leg. Moreover, make sure the hip remains back, or cocked, until the leg touches the imaginary opponent. In this way, the practitioner is prepared to rotate the hips with the subsequent strike. As soon as the foot hits the opponent's leg, the practitioner should drop into a back stance and execute the punch. The speed of this movement accelerates as soon as the foot makes contact with the opponent.*

43 *44* *45*

Chapter 10 — Rohai

46   47   48   49   50

#48. Twist the left leg before executing the crescent kick.

#50. After executing the inside crescent kick, the foot should turn all the way around in the air.

51   52   53   54   55

#51. Notice that Sensei Ota lands with the foot turned in order to execute the shuto. Pull the weight down after the crescent kick.

#53–55. The entire sequence, beginning with the crescent kick and finishing with the second shuto, should be one continuous movement. The first block with the right arm is made with just the arm. There is no body or hip power on the first shuto, just the second. The practitioner is simply trying to establish the distance needed to make a powerful block of the imaginary opponent's second strike in the combination.

Okinawan Karate

56 *57* *58* *59*

#56–57. *Notice how Sensei Ota brings the right arm in before finishing the movement with both arms in front.*

Chapter 10 — Rohai

11
Wanshu

Wanshu kata was introduced into the Tomari district of Okinawa in 1683 by a Chinese envoy or "Sappushi" of that name. Sappushi were the official governmental contacts between China and Okinawa. Following Wanshu, there is nearly a century gap until our knowledge of the development of karate resurfaces with Kung Shang K'ung, also called Kusanku. The opening posture is unique to this form. The ready positions in all other Shorin-ryu kata are quite different than the ready position in Wanshu. However, this position is consistent with many opening salutations in Chinese-style forms. Historically, these postures were ways of identifying and differentiating between specific organizations. According to Grandmaster Nagamine, the hidden fist strike is the signature technique of this kata.

Wanshu lived and worked in Tomari, and aside from his diplomatic responsibilities, he also instructed a small following of disciples in a style called Shaolin White Crane Fist

Boxing. Wanshu taught the importance of blocking and countering while using evasive foot maneuvers. The practitioner also develops the secrets of taking the opponent up and off his feet and throwing him to the ground. Many believe the original version of Wanshu was much longer than the modern kata, which derives from either Kyan or Itosu. Kyan learned the kata from Maeda, a student and contemporary of Kosaku Matsumora. Itosu, on the other hand, learned the kata from Kosaku Matsumora, but he revised the form and actually taught a longer version of the kata.

#2–3. Twist the body to build the tension. This will uncoil the spring on the subsequent punch.

Chapter 11 — Wanshu

4   5   6   7

8   9   10   11   12

#10–12. *The hidden fist punch is executed in a similar way as the slide-in reverse punch in Wankan. The difference is that in Wanshu, the practitioner turns the shoulder and hips when simultaneously pulling the weight back over the rear leg. Bending the knee creates tension in the legs and turning the upper body creates tension in the hips, thereby squeezing the spring tightly. Sensei Ota suggests that the interpretation of this movement is not really a punch, but a way of establishing distance from the opponent. This interpretation is logical because the next movement involves grabbing the opponent.*

Okinawan Karate

13 14 15 16

#13. *If the practitioner practices Wanshu to train the combination sequences, the preceding interpretation is preferred to a hidden punch interpretation, which is meant to somehow surprise the imaginary opponent.*

#14. *The practitioner's rear leg should step behind the front. Drop the weight on the punch by bending the knee of the front leg. This dramatically increases the power of the strike.*

17 18 19 20

#17–18. *Keep the body weight over the rear leg and push off into the forward stance. Remember the front leg establishes direction and the rear leg establishes the power. This fundamental move is also found in Wankan.*

Chapter 11 — Wanshu

21   22   23   24

25   26   27   28   29

#29. This strike is worthy of mention because it is one of the few times in the Matsubayashi-ryu kata curriculum in which an open palm strike is used. This ostensibly points to the Chinese origins of Wanshu. When employing percussive blows of this nature, generally they are targeted at the soft areas of the body or internal organs. Conversely, punching techniques are generally aimed at bones or specific pressure points.

Okinawan Karate

30   31   32

33   34   35   36

37   38   39   40

Chapter 11 — Wanshu

#41. When stepping forward, keep the back arm or the chambered arm tight against the body. Then the arm crosses over the other arm. The blocking arm is always on the outside. This holds for **43** and **45**.

#42–44. When stepping from horse stance to horse stance, try to keep the same height level. This holds for **44–46**.

#47. Twist the upper body to build the tension in the body. Unleash the tension on the ensuing block.

51 52 53 54

#51–54. This sequence is very similar to the ending sequence in Rohai. In Rohai, the difference is that the practitioner executes a crescent kick. In Wanshu, the practitioner executes a throw of some sort. Together these two kata develop one of the most important basic skills for confronting multiple attackers at the same time. That skill is how to turn around quickly while maintaining balance and keeping the spring coiled tight. The right leg should turn all the way around in the air. When the foot lands, it is already fully turned. Before turning, start to bend the knee on the supporting leg. This makes is it easier to maintain balance on the turn. This key skill is also addressed many times in Pinan kata and Fukyukata I.

55 56 57

Chapter 11 — Wanshu

12
Passai

The composer of this kata is unknown, but Passai has long been cherished by karatemen from both Shuri and Tomari and was a particular favorite of Chotoku Kyan. Indeed, the Shuri-te and Tomari-te versions of this form are discernably similar, but which version pre-dates the other is uncertain. Most historians, however, ascribe to the theory that Passai derives from the Soken Matsumura tradition.

Translated into English, Passai means "to breach a fortress." Passai develops skills for fighting at night and grappling, but most importantly, the mental confidence "to thrust asunder." Passai mentally demands that the practitioner make a quantum leap from any kata preceding it in Matsubayashi-ryu. For example, Pinan kata develops a peaceful mind, the ability to relax and still be extremely alert.

The strategy of Pinan is to establish an angle outside the opponent's power line, then block and counterattack. Conversely, the strategy of Passai is to move directly into the line of attack to break down the opponent's attack or "fortress." The Pinan strategy is far less risky and allows for a much greater margin of error. For that reason, Pinan is ideal for beginners, while Passai is reserved for more advanced students. Grandmaster Nagamine noted that Kyan never retreated in a fight, but rather stepped forward or to the side and then counterattacked. Perhaps that was why Passai was his favorite form.

In the Matsubayashi-ryu genealogy, Passai comes through Chotoku Kyan. The Matsubayashi-ryu version of Passai uses many open-handed techniques similar to other Tomari-te versions of the kata. Kyan learned several versions of this form: Matsumura-Passai, Oyadomari-Passai and Matsumora-Passai, and it has been suggested that his personal version reflects elements of all three.

Chapter 12 — Passai

1 2 3 4

#2–4. *The step with the left foot is performed slowly as the practitioner tests the relationship of distance between himself and the opponent. As soon as it is clear that the opponent is reacting, the practitioner leaps forward to block at full speed. The feeling and timing of this movement is similar to Rohai, except the defensive movement in Rohai is to evade the attack by stepping back. In Passai, the practitioner leaps into the attack aggressively to block. This movement is extremely difficult because the practitioner is required to leap and cover a substantial amount of distance and yet come to a complete stop while balancing in a kosa-dachi or cross-legged stance to execute the reinforced block. This movement is both mentally and physically more advanced and more challenging than anything which preceeds it in earlier forms.*

5 6 7

179

Okinawan Karate

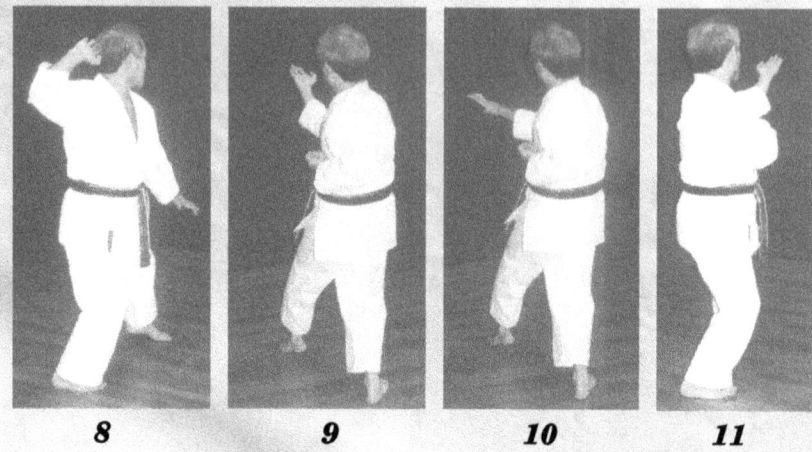

8   9   10   11

#8. *As soon as the toes of the right foot touch the floor, the practitioner should drop his weight into a cat stance and simultaneously block with the right arm. When stepping, the practitioner should bring his right arm and shoulder back. This cocks the hips and coils the spring for the ensuing block.*

#9. *The hips should rotate around fully to build up tension to prepare for the ensuing strike with the left arm. Twisting the hips with the right hand block coils the spring again, so that it generates more speed and power when the left arm strikes to the throat.*

#10. *The right hand grabs the imaginary opponent's arm and pulls. Even if there is no opportunity to grab and pull, the practitioner must guide the opponent's arm down to make room for the striking hand.*

#11. *When the left hand strikes, simultaneously drop the weight into a back stance. Dropping the weight makes it easier to control the opponent and pull the person off balance. The hips rotate back to the original position on the strike. According to Sensei Ota, many practitioners keep their shoulders square and thus cannot rotate the hips. Moreover, many practitioners do not change their height by dropping the weight on the strike. The combination of these fundamental body mechanics helps to generate substantially more speed and power on the block and strike. The body mechanics for this combination are similar to the mechanics in the opening movements in Pinan I.*

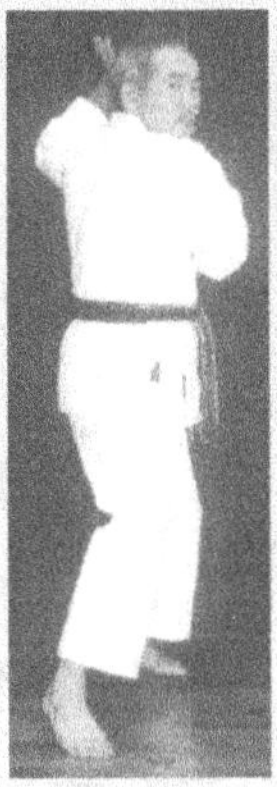
12
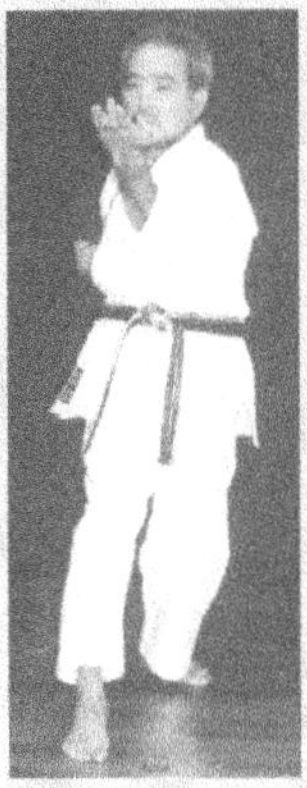
13
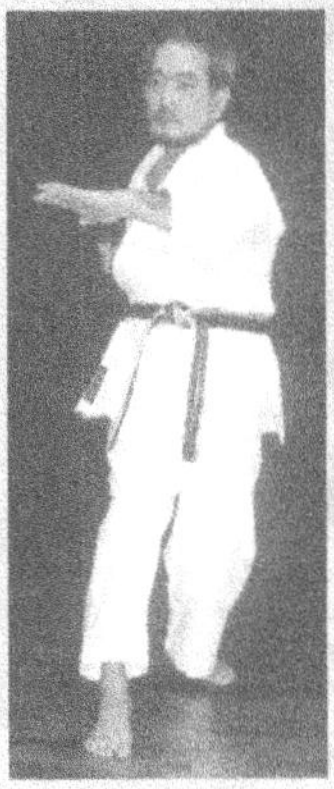
14
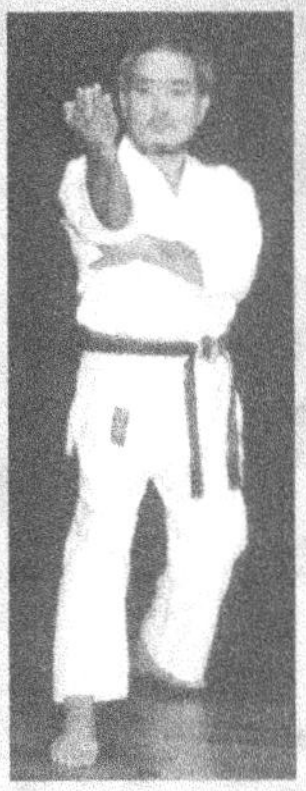
15

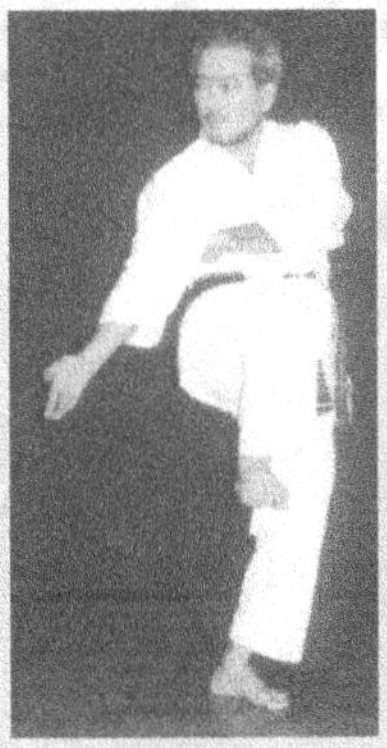
16
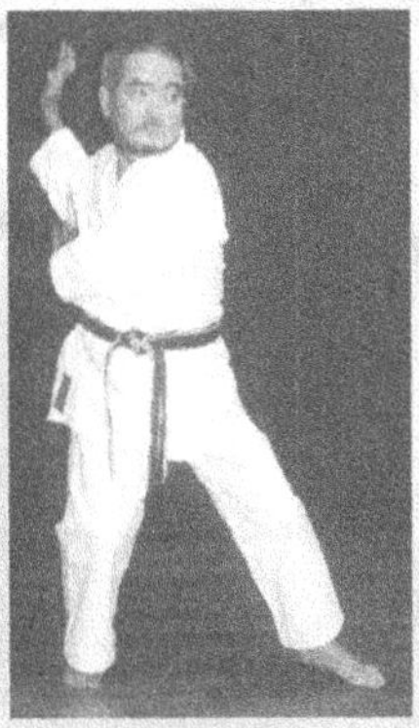
17
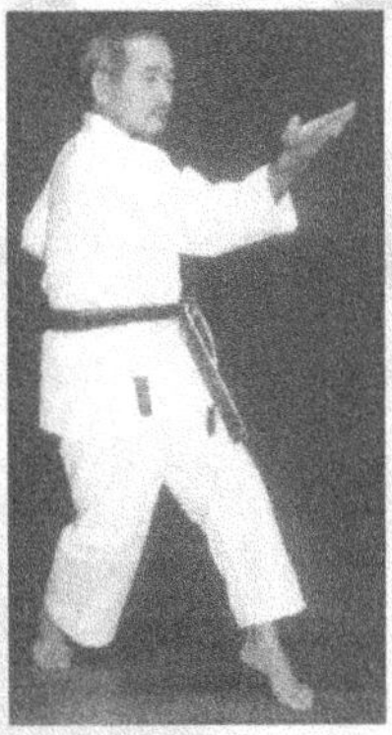
18
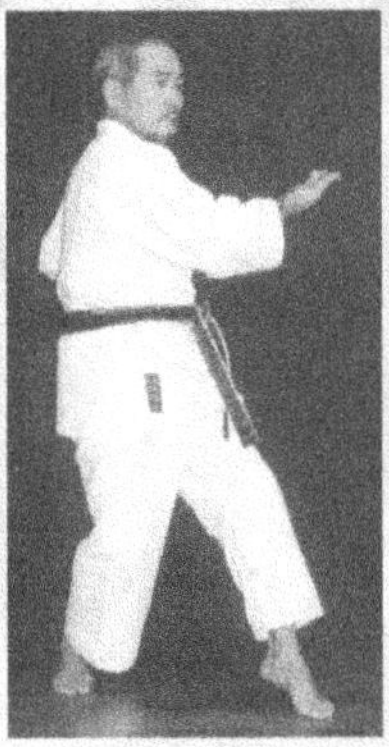
19
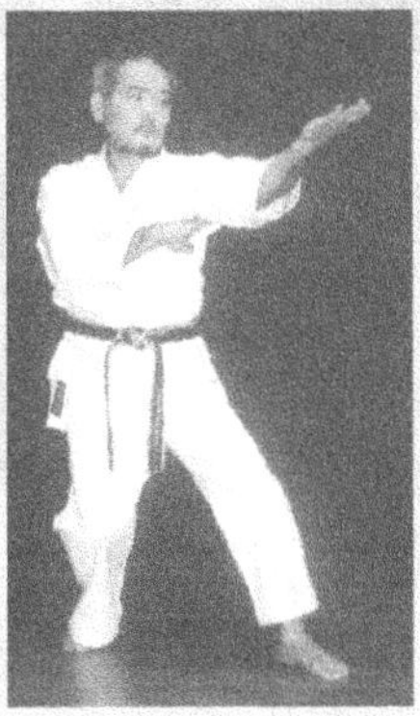
20

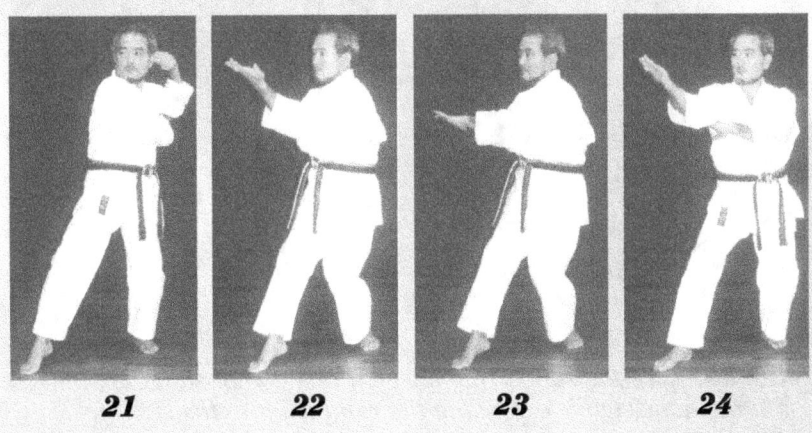

#17. *Upon landing, the practitioner should already have the weight dropped and the body tension coiled.*

21
22
23
24

Okinawan Karate

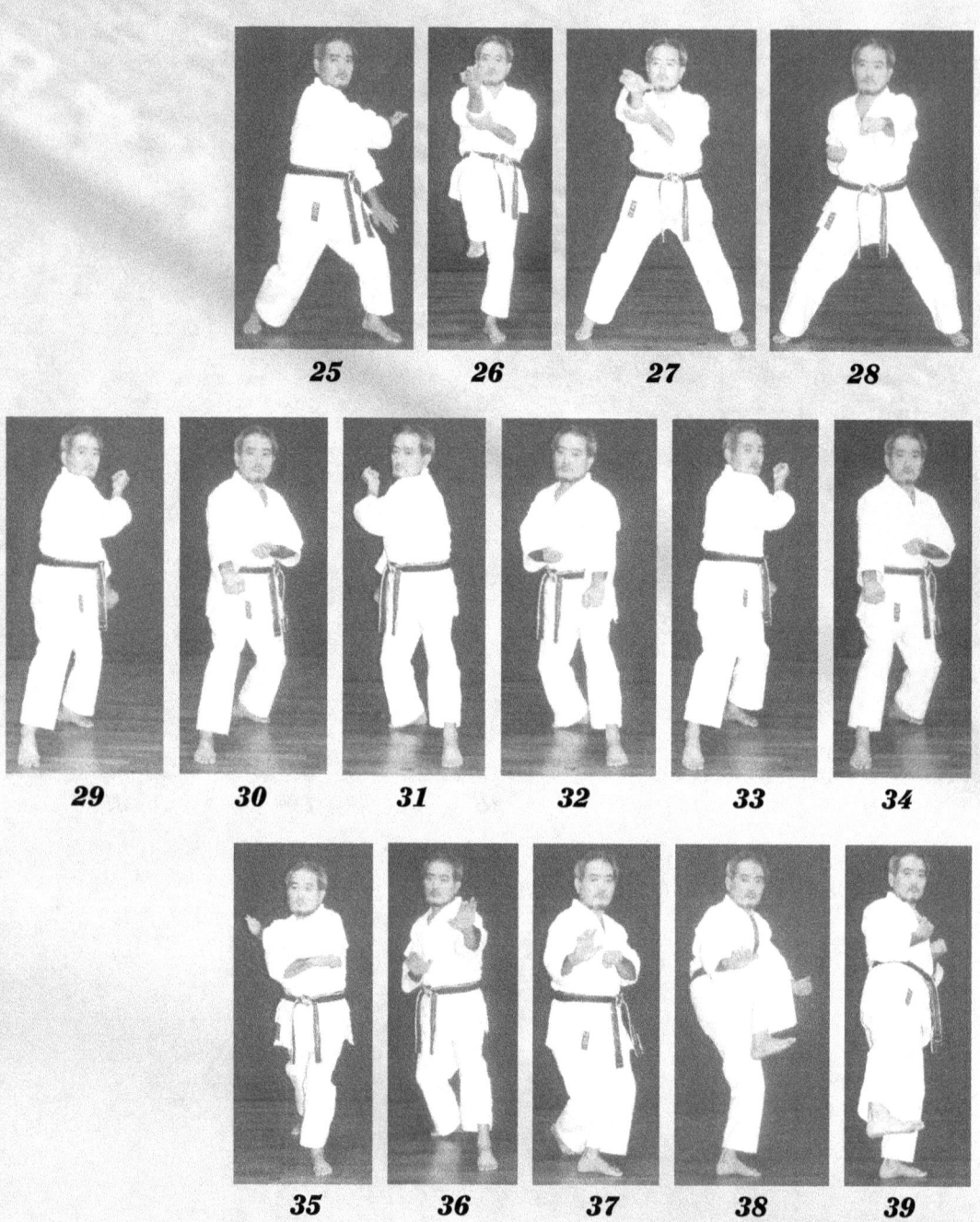

#38–39. Keep the supporting leg bent and do not stand up. Pull with the hands while extending the right leg into the side kick.

Chapter 12 — Passai

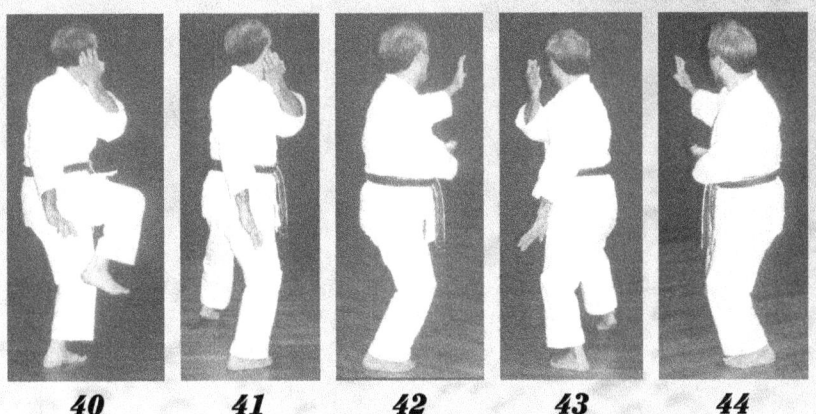

#40–41. When the practitioner turns around to face an imaginary opponent attacking from behind, the turn is also the same as in the beginning of Pinan I. The practitioner should turn his foot in the air and land in the proper stance when the foot hits the ground.

#45–46. When executing the double-rising blocks, sink down lower in the back stance, then strike to the ribs. Drop the body weight to adjust to the opponent's attack. Sinking down is analogous to catching a baseball in a glove. When catching a ball, it is important to have "soft" hands. To prevent the ball from striking the glove with full force, the hand pulls the glove back with the ball to soften the impact. It is the same principle with blocking techniques. Sinking down in the stance is like having "soft" hands.

#47. Cock the right shoulder to build tension before punching.

Okinawan Karate

#54. *Push off the right leg to generate power through the hips, just like in Pinan V.*

Chapter 12 — Passai

57 58 59 60 61

#57–61. *These movements must be performed as one sequence. Following the elbow strike, the practitioner must drop the weight when lowering the right arm. On the set up for the next move, the body weight moves back up. Twist the body to create tension. Twisting the body automatically elevates the practitioner's height. The weight then drops again on the last punch. The practitioner should finish the combination in the standing position.*

62 63 64 65

#62–63. *This move is searching for an opponent and is also discussed in the section on Rohai. Search as far as possible and control the balance by bending the knee of the supporting leg. The hips must stay back to keep the tension in the hips. The tension is released on the double punch. This holds for **66–67** and **70–71**.*

Okinawan Karate

66 67 68 69

70 71 72

Chapter 12 — Passai

73   74   75

#73–74. *This movement refers back to other kata in which turning is discussed in greater detail. Like in all other kata, the practitioner must twist on the right leg or supporting leg. By bending the knee, tension is created in the leg joints. Then the practitioner should push off to develop speed when turning to face an opponent attacking from another direction. In street situations, learning to change direction and turn around quickly is a quintessential skill.*

76   77

#76. *Do not open the arm in preparing for the block on the opposite side. Keep the arm tight against the body.*

187

Okinawan Karate

#78–85. These movements enable you to search for an opponent in the darkness. The foot searches in a circular arc, similar to the way the leg searches for an opponent in Rohai. It is important to reach as far as possible with both the leg and the arm. However, when the arm is searching, the practitioner must keep the ribs covered with the other hand. The arm reaches out slowly, while the other arm is positioned to protect the ribs. Once that arm makes contact with the opponent, the hand grabs and pulls. The power, however, is derived from the hips, not the arm. The practitioner should cover 135 degrees of arc when turning to the left and 180 degrees when searching to the right. Most practitioners cannot cover that amount of distance because they have not developed the necessary skills to turn and change direction in their stances. It is critical to learn to control the joints to execute these searching movements properly.

Chapter 12 — Passai

13
Gojushiho

The composer of this kata is unknown, but modern versions trace back to either Itosu or Kyan. According to most historians, Kyan learned versions of this kata from Matsumura of Shuri and Oyadomari of Tomari. The spear hand movements distinguish Gojushiho from other kata. Gojushiho has been labeled the "drunken monk" form because certain movements are designed to appear off balance to the unsophisticated eye. The practitioner, however, should maintain perfect control and balance during execution of these movements. Translated into English, Gojushiho means "the 54 steps."

The 54 steps, however, do not refer to the number of counts or movements in the kata. According to Zenko Heshiki, Kyoshi 7th dan in Matsbayashi-ryu, the 54 steps refer to the concept of 108 Defilements in Buddhist philosophy. These defilements or faults cause both the body and mind to suffer in Buddhist philosophy. When a Buddhist sees numbers that are factors of 108 (54, 36 or 18), according to Heshiki, he is reminded of the Defilements. In Goju-ryu, there are kata like Sepai, which means "18," Sanseru, which means "36," or Superinpei, which means "108." The relatedness of these numbers between kata from different styles is striking and suggests more than pure coincidence. Many Buddhist temples have 108 steps leading to the shrine. As each of these steps are climbed, a defilement is eliminated. By the time the shrine is reached, the seeker is symbolically cleansed and prepared for enlightenment. Perhaps in the same way, as the karateman practices Gojushiho, he is symbolically polishing his spirit to receive the true benefits of karate training.

The notable historian, Patrick McCarthy, has stated, "The historical Chinese premise which karate kata traces its roots surrounds 36 habitual acts of physical violence and 72 variations for a total of 108 application principles, systematized into a tradition called Louhan Quanfa (Monk Fist Boxing)." One hundred eight divided by 2 equals 54.

#2. *Before executing the backfist with the right hand, the left arm pushes the opponent's punching arm down, similar to a parry.*

#5. *When executing the double-rising blocks in the cat stance, drop the weight. Again, the same analogy of having soft hands when catching a baseball in Passai applies here in Gojushiho.*

Chapter 13 — Gojushiho

#13. *Following the front snap kick with the rear leg, it is critical to finish the kick with the correct weight distribution. When the practitioner lands in the back stance, the weight should be over the rear leg and the body should be coiled and ready to spring forward, as opposed to having to adjust the weight distribution after the kick. This move is like the one in Pinan IV, except that in Pinan IV the practitioner executes a double-punch combination.*

193

Okinawan Karate

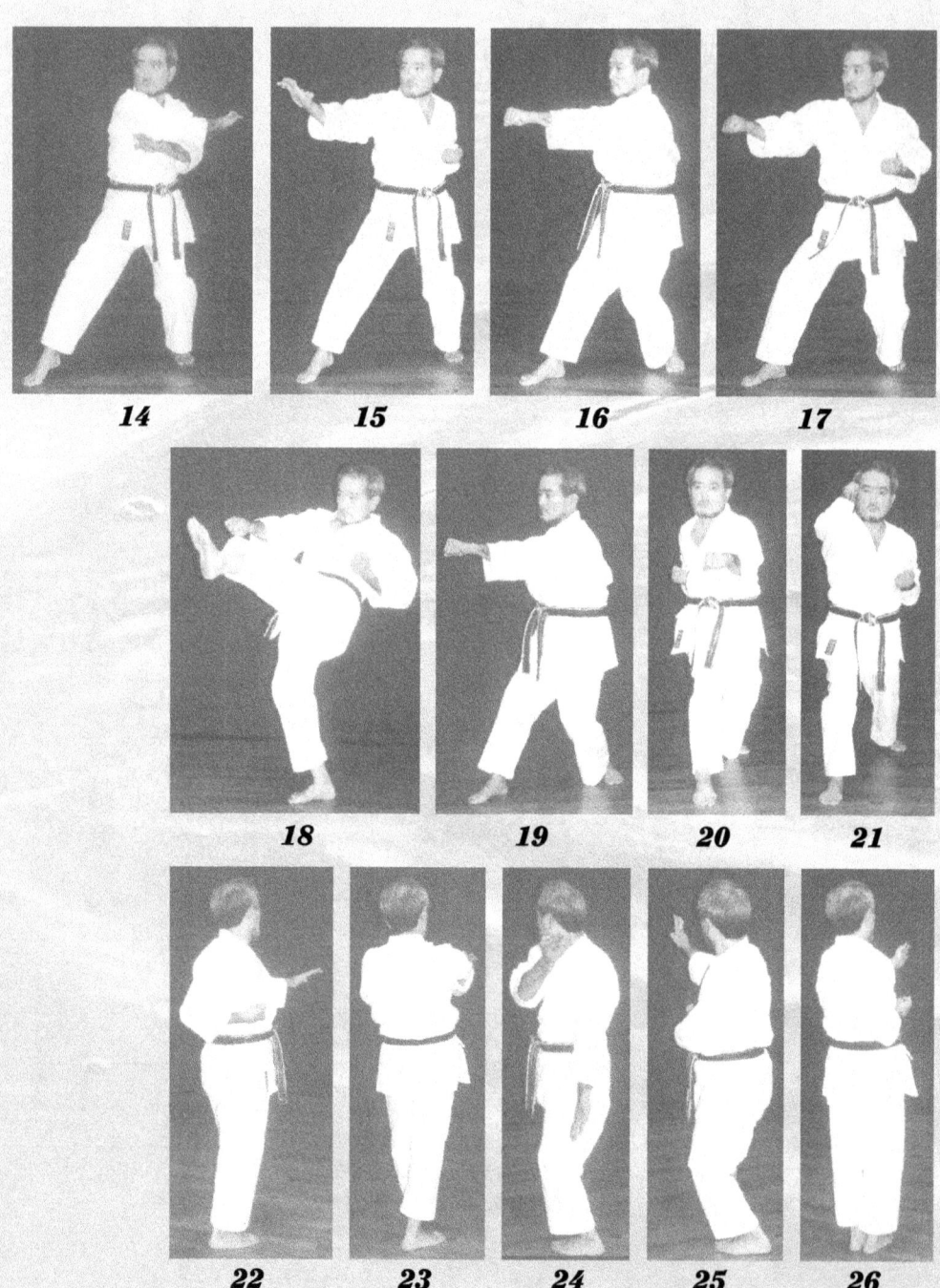

#22. *As the practitioner turns around, he must set up for the next move and coil the spring.*

Chapter 13 — Gojushiho

27 *28* *29* *30*

#27–31. *In this sequence, the practitioner is stepping forward and continually blocking the opponent's attacks by moving his hands in a circular motion. For the last move, the practitioner's left hand should be guarding the middle of the chest. This sequence of moves using multiple spear hand blocks is unique to Gojushiho.*

31

Okinawan Karate

32 33 34 35 36

#34–36. *The block and punch should be one combination, and the practitioner should not pause in between. When the practitioner steps forward and executes this combination and the two subsequent combinations, he should maintain a level height. This holds for **37–39**.*

37 38 39

Chapter 13 — Gojushiho

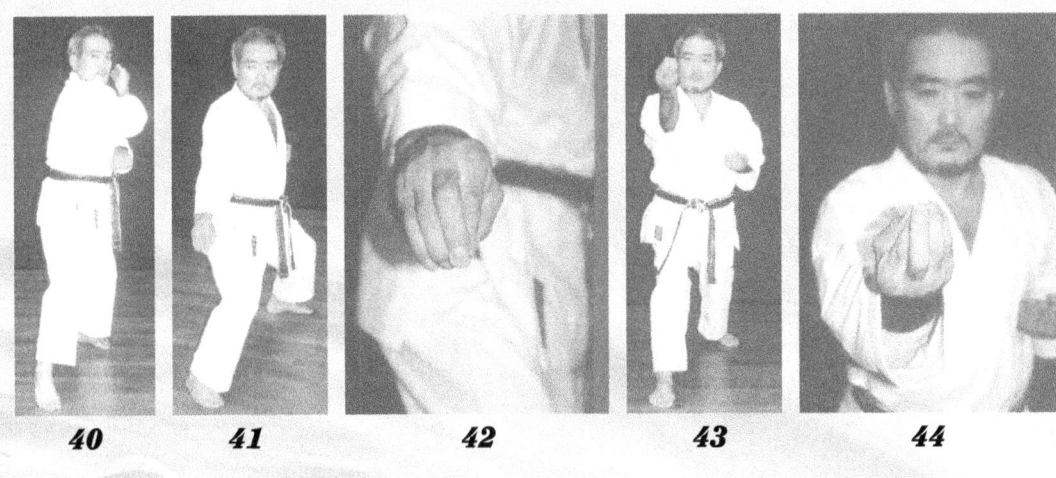

40 41 42 43 44

45 46 47 48 49 50

#48–50. *Sensei Ota performs this movement by executing a simultaneous double backfist. In Grandmaster Nagamine's book, the simultaneous double backfist is left out. Sensei Ota learned the kata this way, but it may have been changed several times over the years. Sensei Ota continues to practice the way he was taught. The concern is simply to point out an important application, which for one reason or another, was deleted from Grandmaster's rendition of Gojushiho in* The Essence of Okinawan Karate-do.

Okinawan Karate

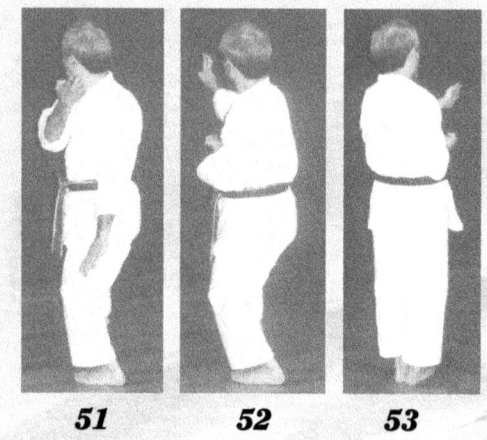

51 52 53

54 55 56 57

Chapter 13 — Gojushiho

58 59

60 61 62

#59–62. *These sequences in which the practitioner appears to fall off balance and then recover to deliver a strike with the fingers is sometimes likened to the "drunken monk" forms in Chinese martial arts. It is critical, however, that the practitioner maintain perfect balance and control at all times. To do this most effectively, the leg that is in the air must come down and touch the floor as quickly as possible to establish balance. The first part of the movement, in which the practitioner leans on one leg, is performed slowly as if intoxicated, but the rest of the movement is performed with speed and dexterity.*

Okinawan Karate

63 *64* *65* *66* *67*

Chapter 13 — Gojushiho

#68–69. *The practitioner is pushing the opponent's punch down with the left hand and counter attacking with a backfist, which is executed with the right arm.*

#71. *The practitioner in this movement steps backwards to establish distance. There is not a lot of twisting or power on the technique. The purpose is to stop the opponent's momentum, while power is delivered on the subsequent punch.*

Okinawan Karate

79 80 81

#80-81. *In this sequence, the practitioner pulls back into a cat stance. Then he must step forward and thrust both arms while remaining in a cat stance. It is important that the practitioner maintains a level height throughout the movement.*

82 83 84 85

Chapter 13 — Gojushiho

14
Chinto

The composer of this kata is unknown, but we know the form was the favorite of Ankichi Arakaki. Chinto means "fighting to the East," and the embusen, or pattern for the kata, is performed in a straight line ... though it is in a diagonal from the opening stance. Most versions of Chinto derive from one of the following: Matsumura of Shuri, who used a straight forward and back embusen; Matsumora of Tomari, who used a side to-side embusen; or Chotoku Kyan, who used a diagonal embusen. The Kyan version of Chinto clearly traces its origins back to the Tomari-te kata of Matsumora. The Matsubayashi-ryu version of Chinto comes directly from Kyan.

Chinto kata is characterized by its dynamic movements and kicking techniques, including the flying front kick. Chinto contains many changes of direction all along the same straight line pattern and requires an advanced level of skill and balance to perform properly. The signature movement in which the right arm moves in a backwards, circular movement is performed three times during the kata. The verb "to invite" in Japanese provides insight into the application of this movement in the kata. Indeed, many kata contain movements that suggest an invitation to the opponent to attack.

Okinawan Karate

#3–5. This movement is similar to the movement in Ananku. The right arm should move around in a circular motion at a slow and deliberate speed. As soon as the right arm comes fully around and touches the left arm, the next move should be executed at full speed. Sensei Ota's interpretation of this movement is to invite the opponent to attack. By moving the arm, it gives the appearance to the opponent that the defenses are down and that the practitioner is vulnerable to attack. Hence, the practitioner is inviting the opponent to attack.

Chapter 14 — Chinto

10   *11*

12   *13*   *14*   *15*

#11. *Sensei Ota argues that this position in Chinto is not a simultaneous double block in which the practitioner blocks a kick from an attacker in front and a head-level punch from an attacker in the rear. To Sensei Ota, that is a very unrealistic interpretation. The better interpretation is that the back arm is holding the opponents at bay. This position psychologically sends a signal to the opponents that the practitioner is aware of their presence and ready to deal with a potential attack.*

#12–14. *Twist the right foot before spinning around. Keep the leg close to the body or it will be extremely difficult for the practitioner to execute this movement with speed and still maintain balance. If the practitioner loses balance, it is impossible to execute the ensuing lower block. When the practitioner lands, he must already have his body coiled and ready to block.*

#19–21. The flying kick is worthy of mention because it is rare to see a flying kick anywhere in Okinawan karate. Typically, the practitioner roots himself to the ground. The flying kick, however, was a favorite of Kyan. Many practitioners perform this as a flying double kick. But, as with most karate combinations, the second strike delivers the true power and the purpose of the first kick is to set up the finishing technique. In this case, the first kick is more of a fake to create the opening for the second kick.

Chapter 14 — Chinto

22 23 24 25

#22. *It is important that the practitioner learn to bring his weight down following the flying kick. Make sure to cock the arms to coil the spring before thrusting the arms in the next movement.*

26 27 28

209

Okinawan Karate

29 *30*

#30. Following the elbow strike in the forward stance, the practitioner adjusts his stance by pulling back to a cat stance and adjusting the hands like a shuto. However, the arms are not chambered like a normal shuto movement. Rather the shuto is shortened and executed without chambering the arms. This idea is similar to the way the shuto are executed at the end of Rohai and Wanshu.

31 *32* *33* *34*

Chapter 14 — Chinto

35 36 37 38

#35–36. *Step out with the right foot. Generate power on the next move by turning the entire body. Do not just swing the arms. Use the left leg to control the uncoiling of the spring. The right arm crosses over. Keep the arm close to the body to set up for the double-arm technique.*

39 40 41 42 43

211

Okinawan Karate

44 45 46 47

48 49 50 51

#48. Drop the weight when the hands drop to the legs. This will build tension to move faster on the ensuing technique, like the coiling of a spring.

#49. This punch is not a shortened punch with the fist held straight the way it is pictured in Nagamine's book. Rather, the punch should be fully extended and pulled back after the punch. The elbow, however, is held out because the practitioner is blocking first, then sliding the arm in to strike the opponent. Sensei Ota refers to this technique as a simultaneous "blocking punch."

Chapter 14 — Chinto

52 *53* *54* *55* *56*

57 *58* *59* *60* *61*

62 *63* *64* *65*

#64. Drop the weight when the hands drop to the legs. This will build tension so the practitioner can move faster on the ensuing technique, like the coiling of a spring.

66 *67* *68* *69*

Chapter 14 — Chinto

#71–73. When moving the arms from an outstretched position together, the arms should move slowly. As soon as the arms touch, move into the next position at full speed.

215

Okinawan Karate

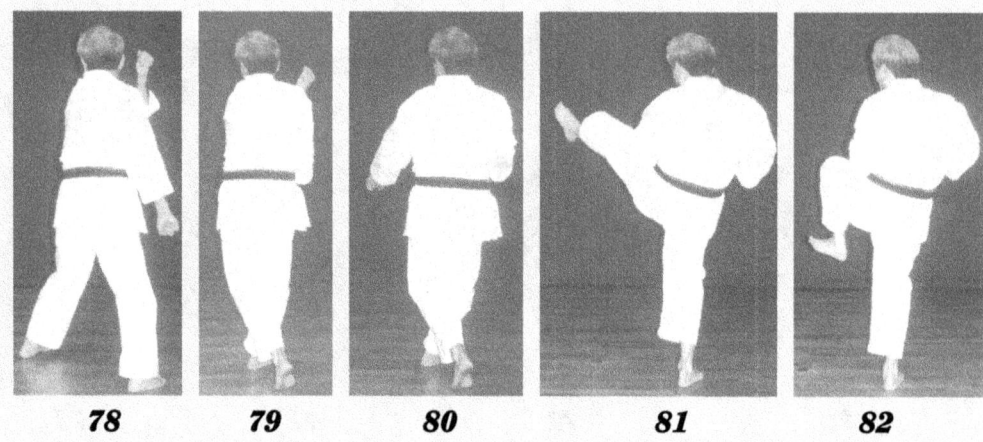

78 79 80 81 82

#82. *Keep the weight down so that you can push off and extend into the next movement.*

83 84 85 86

Chapter 14 — Chinto

87 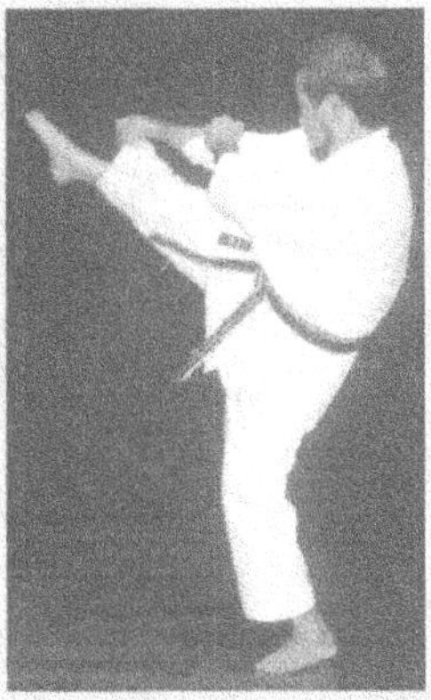 88  89  90

91  92  93  94

95 96

217

15
Kusanku

Kusanku, or "Kanku" in Japanese, can be translated into English as "to view the sky," which is often used to explain the opening movement of the kata. However, according to most experts, Kusanku or, Kung Shang K'ung, was the name of a Chinese military envoy who introduced the kata in Shuri around 1761. Many believe that Kusanku derives from Sokon Matsumura. Kusanku instructed To-de Sakugawa, Matsumura's principal instructor, and Matsumura himself directly. But, Kusanku also trained directly with Chatan Yara, a contemporary of Sakugawa. The very existence of a Yara version would indicate an earlier origin than Matsumura. The Matsubayashi-ryu version of the kata comes down through Chotoku Kyan, who learned the kata from Yomitan Yara, the grandson of Chatan Yara. Kyan also was familiar with with both Matsumura's and Matsumora's versions of the kata. Kusanku was Kyan's favorite form.

According to Grandmaster Nagamine, Kusanku is the most magnificent of all Matsubayashi-ryu kata. It is also the most difficult to perform. The signature stance of

Grandmaster Nagamine

Okinawan Karate

Kusanku, demonstrated on the previous page, is a perfect example of the athleticism required to perform this kata. The practitioner is required to go down to the ground and leap in the air to execute a kick. Kusanku is also the longest kata in Matsubayashi-ryu, and it requires advanced levels of stamina and strength to perform well.

Many experts believe that Itosu based the Pinan series of kata on Kusanku. Clearly many of the same movements are used in Pinan. Therefore, for technical explanations on these important sequences, please refer to the chapter on Pinan kata.

Chapter 15 — Kusanku

6   *7*   *8*

#7. *Step out with the right foot. Cock the arm for the block. Make sure to keep the blocking arm close to the body when cocking the arm.*

9   *10*   *11*   *12*

Okinawan Karate

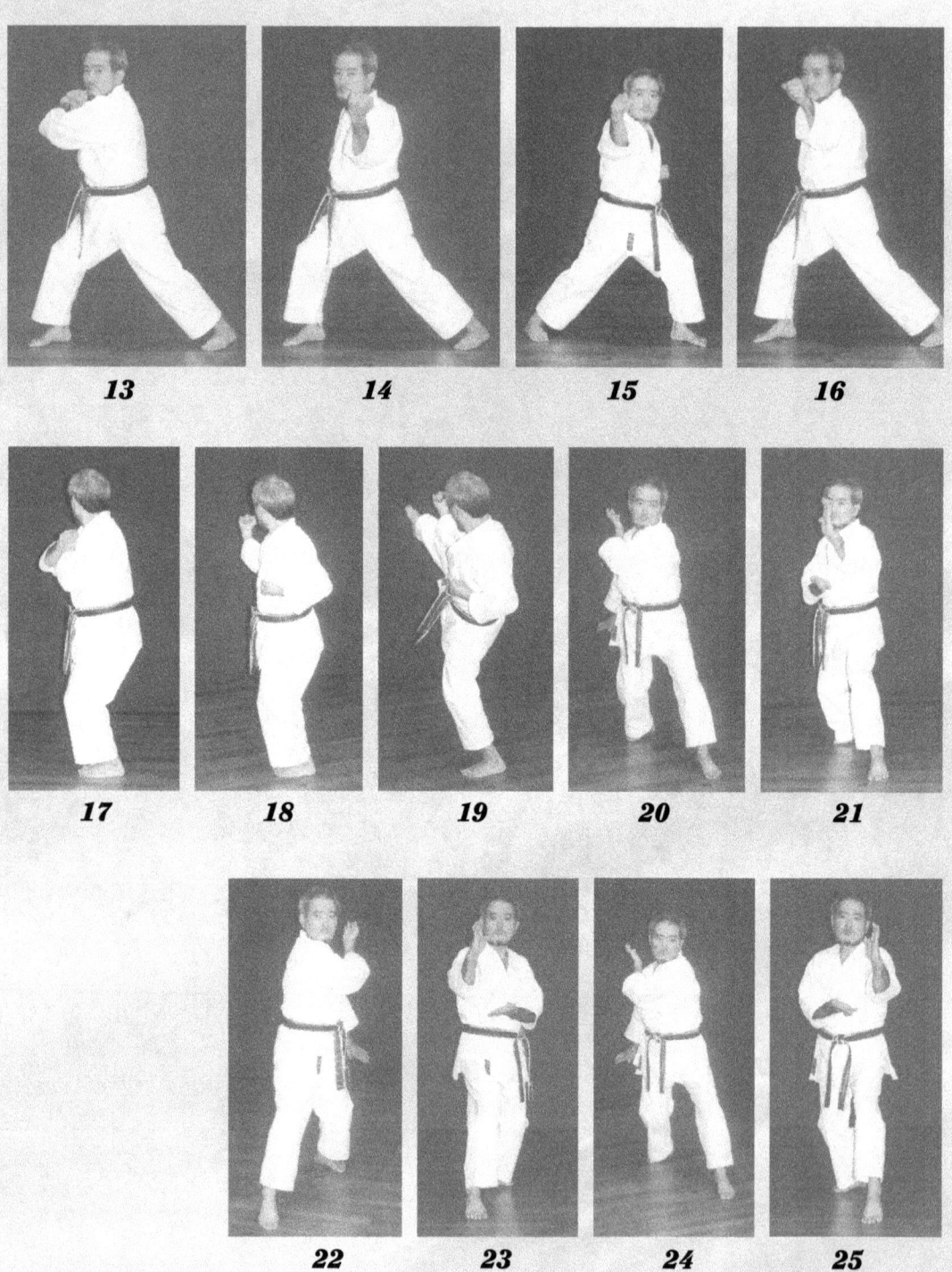

Chapter 15 — Kusanku

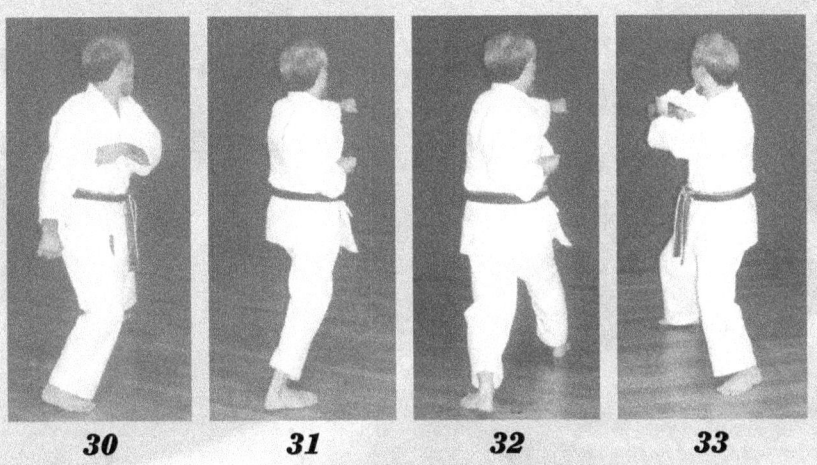

#30. When turning around, the left leg determines the direction. The right leg delivers the power. Drop the weight to build the tension in the right leg before uncoiling the body into the next position. This move is similar to Pinan V and Passai.

#31. Do not twist the body to punch. Rather, the practitioner is establishing distance with the left arm. Snap it out quickly without cocking back for a punch.

Okinawan Karate

#38–39. *This is the signature stance in Kusanku. It is very difficult for most students to get this low in the stance. Generally, either age or injury prevents most students from executing this stance effectively. Indeed, it could easily be more a liability than an asset for a practitioner to try to use this strategy if he cannot pop up out of the low stance quickly enough. The stance invites attack, particularly kicks to the head from an opponent because the practitioner appears very vulnerable to that kind of attack. Begin to stand and block when the opponent initiates an attack.*

Chapter 15 — Kusanku

42 43 44 45

46 47 48

49 50 51 52

Okinawan Karate

53 54 55

56 57 58 59

60 61 62 63

Chapter 15 — Kusanku

64   65   66   67

#65-67. Step out with the right leg. The right arm moves around in a circular, counter clockwise position before finishing the movement.

68   69   70   71

Okinawan Karate

#73–74. The first technique with the right arm is a block, followed by a punch with the left hand. Drop the weight on the punch and make sure the body twists on both the block and punch to generate power.

#75. This move is similar to Naihanchi kata. Drop the weight on this move.

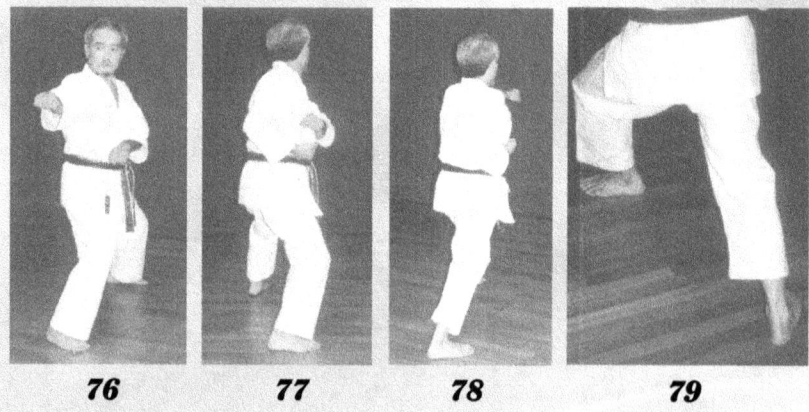

#76–77. Step out with the left leg to determine direction. The right leg generates the power. Coil the spring by dropping the weight over the right leg and uncoil the body on the block.

#78–79. Twist the left leg before the crescent kick, just like in Rohai. Drop the weight when turning around.

Chapter 15 — Kusanku

80 *81* *82*
83 *84* *85* *86*
87 *88* *89* *90*

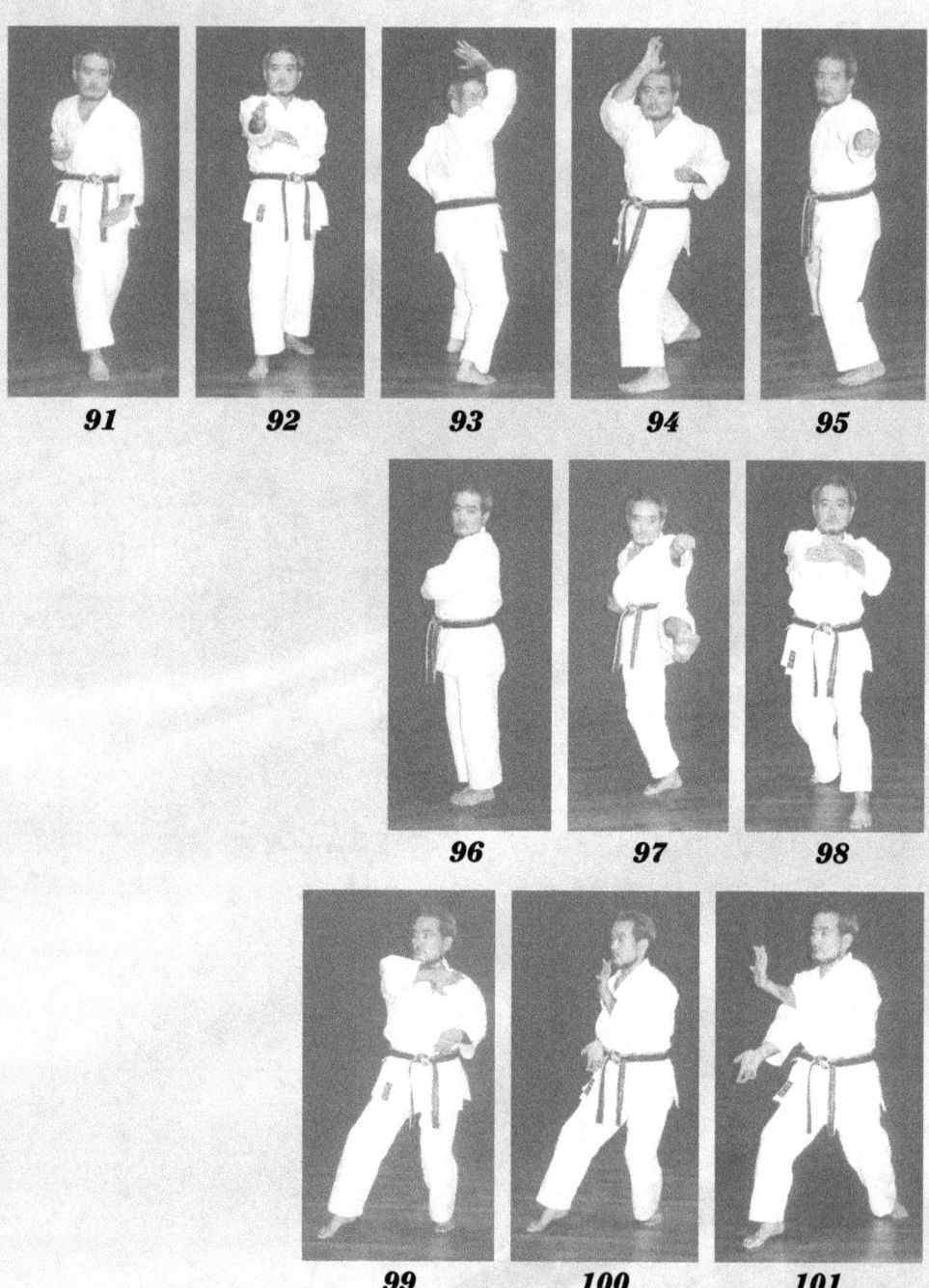

#99–101. *This is one of the rare times in the Matsubayashi-ryu kata curriculum in which the practitioner uses this kind of open-handed technique. It is more commonly used in Naha-te kata curricula.*

Chapter 15 — Kusanku

102   103   104   105   106

107   108   109   110   111

#109–111. Once again the right arm moves around in a circular, counter clockwise movement before the final position.

Okinawan Karate

112 *113* *114* *115* *116*

#114–115. This is another flying kick, similar to the kick in Chinto. Please refer to the chapter on Chinto for a more thorough explanation of the kick's execution.

#116. Following the flying kick, the practitioner must land in a cat stance. It is very difficult to land with the body weight low and the rear leg ready to spring, while maintaining proper balance and posture. The landing of this kick in Kusanku is more difficult than the landing of the same kick in Chinto.

117 *118* *119* *120*

Chapter 15 — Kusanku

121 *122* *123* *124* *125*

Okinawan Karate

Section Three
TRAINING

Chapter 16 — Ikken Hisatsu

16
Ikken Hisatsu

It was during a karate clinic back in 1972 that students witnessed a display of power that still echoes in the halls of that Matsubayashi-ryu dojo in Ohio. The clinic was conducted by two young karate Sensei from Okinawa: Eihachi Ota and Master Takayoshi 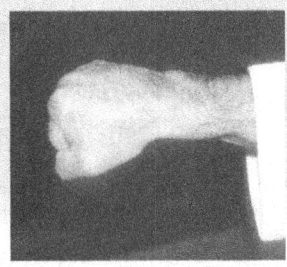 Nagamine, the son of Grandmaster Shoshin Nagamine. Along the wall of the dojo there were four makiwara. While they were warming up, Sensei Ota jokingly said to Takayoshi that he thought he could break the makiwara with a single punch. Takayoshi, in disbelief, called Sensei Ota's bluff and challenged him to break the makiwara. Undaunted, Sensei Ota snapped the first post with a reverse punch almost effortlessly. Immediately 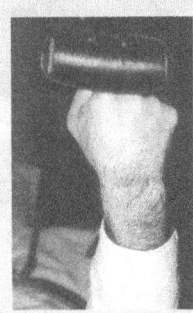 a crowd of students gathered around to see what was happening. The students were each invited to break one of the remaining makiwara if they were able. Several tried unsuccessfully using punches, elbow strikes and even kicks. Then they tried to use their combined strength to break the wooden posts by pulling and bending the wood. Even with their combined strength and weight they were unable to crack the makiwara. Once again, Sensei Ota demonstrated his power by snapping the makiwara with one punch, while the students marveled at his technique. At the time, Sensei Ota stood 5 feet 6 inches tall and weighed about 135 pounds.

In his typical modesty, Sensei Ota downplays the significance of these awesome demonstrations of power. He does caution students that the angle of attack must be absolutely perfect or the practitioner will cause serious injury to himself, especially under the force required to break a makiwara, which can amount to thousands of pounds of pressure. Even the slightest deviation will certainly result in broken bones. Of course, the purpose of makiwara training is not to break the makiwara, but to develop the hands into lethal weapons.

The makiwara has historically always been an essential aspect of Okinawan Karate, which was developed as a means for the people of Okinawa to defend themselves after the Japanese Shogun had banned them from carrying weapons. Grandmaster Nagamine practiced with the makiwara on a daily basis until his death at 90 years of age. Indeed, in *The Essence of Okinawan Karate-Do*, Grandmaster Nagamine asserts, "I do not know of any karate men who do not hit the makiwara."

Sensei Ota has never discontinued his training on the makiwara. Nevertheless, he recognizes that people practice karate for a variety of reasons. Many practitioners train simply to improve their health or physical fitness. To Sensei Ota this is not a problem because there are many positive benefits to karate practice besides developing deadly punching power. The demands of makiwara training are too physically punishing for the average karate student. However, for students who want to develop "battle-ready" punching technique, or Ikken Hisatsu (one punch stopping power), then makiwara practice is *de riguer*.

The makiwara is prevalent in other styles of karate as well. In *Conversations with the Master*, Masatoshi Nakayama, former head of the JKA, when questioned about his training under Master Gichen Funakoshi, replied:

> "The training sessions under Master Funakoshi were very strict and rigid. During class sessions at the university, Funakoshi Sensei would have us perform technique after technique, hundreds of times each. When he selected a kata for us to practice, we would repeat it at least 50 or 60 times, and this was always followed by intense practice on the makiwara, and I can vividly remember him striking the makiwara as many as 1,000 times."

The legendary Choki Motobu, one of Grandmaster Nagamine's instructors, in his book *Okinawan Kempo* explains:

> "The method of using the makiwara developed at the Shuri Castle was unique in at least two aspects, one general and one specific to the exercises themselves. Generally speaking, makiwara training was the central focus point of their daily practice. All other aspects of their training were based on a supposition of knowledge and performance dependent on years of makiwara practice. Specifically the way they hit the makiwara developed a special type of force and control."

Lessons from Makiwara

Many karate students think the purpose of the makiwara is to toughen the hands and knuckles, especially the bones in the hands. According to Sensei Ota, developing "hard hands" is only a by-product of makiwara training, not the main objective. Sensei Ota enjoys pointing out the obvious, "You cannot control your bones. Karate techniques require students to develop control over their muscles and tendons. Your ability to control your own body determines the amount of force or power you are able to deliver."

Makiwara training develops the practitioner's ability to coordinate the contraction and relaxation of specific muscle groups at the precise times to generate maximum power. This is the primary objective of makiwara training.

Choki Motobu poetically wrote:

> "Hitting the makiwara in a method reminiscent of a willow branch snapping in the wind, but holding the final point of contact as firmly as a piece of steel rod for a brief time, developed a type of focused strike easily recognized as the thrusting punch of Karate-Jutsu."

After striking the makiwara for a period of time, students begin to learn by feel how to apply the appropriate amount of force with the shoulder, elbow and wrist. The alignment of these joints is critical, especially at the point of delivery. If the joints are held too tightly, then not enough speed is generated and the resulting force is greatly reduced. Moreover, this can eventually lead to injuries. If the joints in the shoulders, elbows and wrists are too loose, then there is a lack of focus and again the resulting force will be inadequate. Under either of these faulty scenarios, the technique cannot be executed effectively. Makiwara training helps practitioners to develop body control so that they can increase speed and maximize their striking power: This is Ikken Hisatsu.

There are two ways to punch the makiwara. The first is similar to the normal punching motion in which the fist is retracted immediately after contact has been made. Striking the makiwara in this way allows the striking post to vibrate, graphically demonstrating the force of the blow. The movement of the makiwara makes it dramatically more difficult to strike the target in the right place with the correct part of the hand. If the timing is off, injury may result.

The second method of striking the makiwara is to leave the punch extended, maintaining contact with the striking post for a longer duration. This forces the fist to absorb the vibration and requires the practitioner to hold the fist tight for a longer period of time, which develops muscle control at the essential moment of impact. This type of training uses a different rhythm and cadence than the first. Together both techniques develop the foundation for Ikken Hisatsu.

One of the most important lessons Sensei Ota has learned from his years of training on the makiwara is the proper delivery of a strike. By relaxing the muscles immediately after making contact, the amount of force he generates is increased significantly. Without releasing that energy, the force of the strike is severely limited. Sensei Ota asserts that power from the punching technique is derived as much from the action of pulling back as the forward momentum from the thrust. Proper technique results in a quick, snapping blow. Perfecting this kind of technique, however, can take a lifetime to achieve.

Moreover, the speed with which the practitioner pulls back after one technique will determine how fast he can set up for the next. The speed that the practitioner is able to generate on the pull back directly contributes to the speed and therefore to the resulting force of any subsequent moves that are executed in combination.

Conditioning the Hands

An additional purpose of the makiwara is to develop the fists into deadly weapons. This is achieved through repeatedly striking the makiwara until the tendons that pass over the knuckles are pushed off to the sides around the knuckles. After sufficient striking in this manner, the tendons per-

manently adopt this position, enabling the practitioner to strike directly with the bones of the hand, thus protecting the more delicate tendons in the process.

Repeatedly striking the makiwara with enough force to alter the path of the tendons should also cause the skin around the knuckles to tear. The skin will easily tear even after only a few strikes. The skin should be peeled away at the point when this occurs. Practitioners should not stop striking the makiwara until the skin around the knuckles can be entirely removed. After the skin is completely torn away, a second skin begins to form slowly. This process requires multiple repetitions to properly develop the knuckles for striking. Each subsequent skin that grows back is tougher and tighter than the last. This process of tearing the skin away from the knuckles must be repeated several times to achieve the optimal results. Sensei Ota cautions that the knuckles may look rather scary at this point (like something you might expect to see at a butcher's shop), but it is a necessary part of makiwara training. Sensei Ota believes that this is a critical time because many practitioners submit to the pain at this point and quit before fully tearing the skin away from the knuckles.

There are two different kinds of makiwara: those with soft padding and those with hard padding or no padding. Practitioners who train only on soft makiwara, which includes most practitioners in Japan and Okinawa, develop large swollen knuckles covered over by layer upon layer of scar tissue. This scar tissue serves only to cushion the force of the blow and does nothing to harden the fists or to move the delicate tendons out of harm's way. The swollen knuckles can actually prevent the bone from making contact on the makiwara. Sensei Ota tells students that they must use both kinds of makiwara in Ikken Hisatsu.

Chapter 16 — Ikken Hisatsu

Exercises

Close Distance: Karate students should begin by striking the makiwara at a close distance. Place one foot in front of the other and practice the reverse punch on both sides. As practitioners increase their sense of distance and timing, they should begin to increase the twisting of the joints in the hips, knees and shoulders.

Intermediate and Long Distance: When students become proficient striking the makiwara at a close distance, they should begin to move progressively further away from the striking post. Sensei Ota warns that as the distance from the makiwara increases, the difficulty increases exponentially. Accuracy at a long distance away from the makiwara becomes extremely important, yet much more difficult to achieve. Beginning level practitioners will inevitably miss the target and injure their wrists. Yet, they must continue if they are going to develop Ikken Hisatsu for combat situations. The distance in kumite is generally longer than the close distance most people use when training with the makiwara. This is why Sensei Ota practices various exercises that involve shifting footwork when practicing from intermediate and longer distances from the makiwara.

243

Okinawan Karate

Spinning Technique: Sensei Ota also practices striking the makiwara while turning around in a spinning motion. This generates even greater speed and force. In this way, Sensei Ota is also able to use the momentum generated by the coordinated movements of the entire body. Practitioners must develop control over all the joints in the body to control their accuracy, especially when spinning around to strike.

Training with a Partner: Sensei Ota recommends that practitioners train in pairs. When students begin makiwara practice, the pain can often be overwhelming and they soon give up. But, when practicing with a partner, students can help to inspire each other to go further, using each other's rhythm and pace to challenge themselves. Indeed, the rhythmical sounds of trading punches increases concentration and focus. Students should start by facing each other, on either side of the makiwara, each having the outside foot forward,

and begin trading reverse punches, one with the left hand and the other with the right hand. After a while the students should change sides to develop the other hand.

Kicking: While most makiwara training is directed at developing hand techniques, the feet and proper kicking technique may also be effectively developed by training with the makiwara.

Other Strikes: Students can also develop open-handed striking and blocking techniques by training on the maikwara as well, and they can also be practiced in combination with other fighting techniques.

Makiwara training is overlooked by the majority of karate dojo, which Sensei Ota has observed over the past 30 years in America. Although he readily admits that it is essential to the development of Ikken Hisatsu, Sensei Ota recognizes that there are many benefits to karate training, and he does not insist that his students practice on the makiwara. There are many other benefits derived from makiwara training as well, just as there are many benefits derived from karate training itself. Sensei Ota recognizes that most practitioners are not willing to risk the bodily injury that inevitably results from serious makiwara training, so he prefers to leave the decision open to each individual student. The makiwara in Sensei Ota's dojo are always right on the main floor, but everyone is left to address them on his own terms. Sensei Ota does not include makiwara training as part of the regular group class curriculum, but makiwara is always encouraged as an extra-curricular necessity.

Chapter 16 — Ikken Hisatsu

17
Tsumasaki Geri

Shorin-ryu's forgotten toe-tip kick

In one of the most comprehensive texts ever written about the art of karate, the notable historian and prolific writer John Sells, in *Unante: The Secrets of Karate* states:

"The Okinawans favoured certain specific striking techniques such as the toe-tip technique that is virtually unseen in today's tournament style karate. The tip of the toes or tsumasaki was considered a superior weapon with which to strike the opponent. A kick was snapped suddenly and fiercely with the toes extended thoroughly concentrating the power. This kick is still practiced in Okinawan styles though is almost never seen in Japan and elsewhere."

The toe-tip kick also seems to be an innovation of karate men from the Shorin-ryu lineages. Though it may be taught in various Naha-te styles, it was the Shorin-ryu practitioners who are remembered for popularizing the technique. In *The Essence of Okinawan Karate-Do*, Nagamine refers to tsumasaki geri in his discussion of the great Ankichi Arakaki (1899–1927). He says, "The story is not complete without describing, albeit briefly, his speciality in Waza." Nagamine continues by stating, "His constant and strenuous efforts, combined with his enthusiasm, would have brought him world recognition as a master of karate and inventor of his unique tsumasaki-geri (toe-tip kick)."

Nagamine further expounds, "After a year of total dedication to the training of nidan-geri (flying front kick) and tsumasaki-geri (toe-tip kick), Arakaki mastered his own unique style of tsumasaki-geri. No other karate man could match his speed and power in this technique." Nagamine continues by providing two accounts of Arakaki using his toe-tip kick in actual street fighting encounters, illustrating the practical application of this technique.

Sensei Ota is one of the few teachers outside Okinawa who teaches tsumasaki geri to his students, and he genuinely believes the technique to be essential for actual combat situations. According to Sensei Ota, front snap kicks in which contact is made with the ball of the foot cannot create the same penetration that tsumasaki geri can. Tsumasaki geri requires the practitioner to have pinpoint accuracy, which allows for attacks to vital areas of the body and specific nerve points. Normal front kicks in which the toes are pulled back and contact is made with the balls of the feet create too much surface area to attack nerve 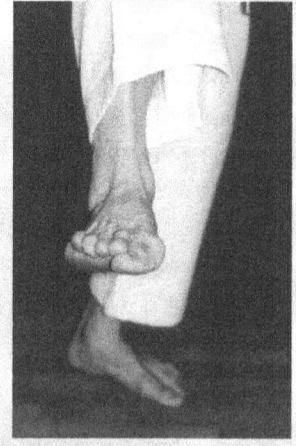 points or the solar plexus or even to areas of the body located deep within the muscle tissues. Normal front kicks can still be effective, especially when attacking the bony areas of the body.

Chapter 17 — Tsumasaki Geri

However, according to Sensei Ota, tsumasaki geri techniques are far more disabling.

Some fighters can endure painful blows from a normal front snap kick and may continue in combat situations even with broken bones. Moreover, when simultaneously facing multiple attackers, the preferable kick is tsumasaki geri. In these situations, disabling an opponent quickly and permanently can be critical.

Sensei Ota explains that tsumasaki geri has long been believed to be a necessary technique for street situations by karate men from around the district of Tomari and has been tested countless times in actual fights. Today Sensei Ota is best known in Shorin-ryu circles for his extensive kumite experience. Perhaps more than any karate man since Choki Motobu, he has proven the validity of his deadly techniques in actual combat situations.

Sensei Ota emphasizes that the main objective of karate study is the development of character, but for those who also wish to be competent fighters, techniques like tsumasaki geri can lead to quantum advancements in combat situations. Sensei Ota still cautions students, however, that the steps necessary to developing the toe-tip kick can be long and painful. Yet, Sensei Ota reminds us that in the days when he was living and training in Okinawa, karate practice was always very severe and strenuous. When delivering a toe-tip kick, explains Sensei Ota, the practitioner does not need to produce as much power as normal snap kicks. However, because the toe-tip kick is designed to attack smaller areas of the opponent's body, the practitioner must rely upon speed and accuracy.

Sensei Ota, like several of his Shorin-ryu predecessors, has made innovations to tsumasaki geri. Sensei Ota prefers to deliver the roundhouse or wheel kick using the tips of the toes instead of either the instep, the balls of the feet or the shins. An important target area using the roundhouse kick is the opponent's throat. Sensei Ota explains that the toes can easily pen-

etrate and disable an opponent and so too can a kick to the solar plexus or between individual ribs. Ordinarily, the roundhouse kick is far less powerful than other kicks. Mostly, the roundhouse kick is used by tournament fighters that need not concern themselves with issues like the practicality of their techniques. The roundhouse gives the tournament fighter alternative angles to attack the opposing fighter. But, if the roundhouse kick is delivered with the tip of the toes, it also becomes a deadly weapon.

Conditioning the Toes

Sensei Kazuo Tajima, Kyoshi 7th dan, is currently part of the Kishaba-jiku organization and is Master Kishaba's most senior student after Sensei Shinzato. Sensei Tajima explains

Chapter 17 — Tsumasaki Geri

that practitioners must develop flexibility in their toes and feet to properly execute tsumasaki geri. Below are various exercises, demonstrated by Sensei Tajima, that students should practice to condition their toes:

1. Stand on a step or stairs and bend the toes forward and back over the front edge. Hyperextending the toes helps to increase pliability in the joints.

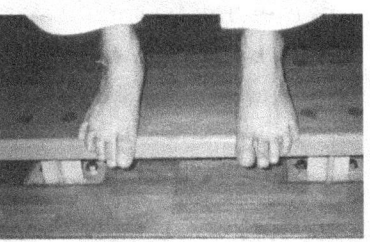

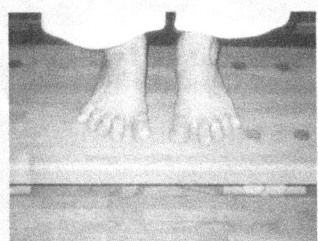

2. Open and close the toes. Try to open the toes as widely as possible while gripping the floor each time the toes are opened. This exercise not only enhances flexibility, but builds strength in the toes as well.

3. Move to the edge of a step or stairs and do toe raises up and down to increase strength. Begin with all five toes, then move to three toes and ultimately just one.

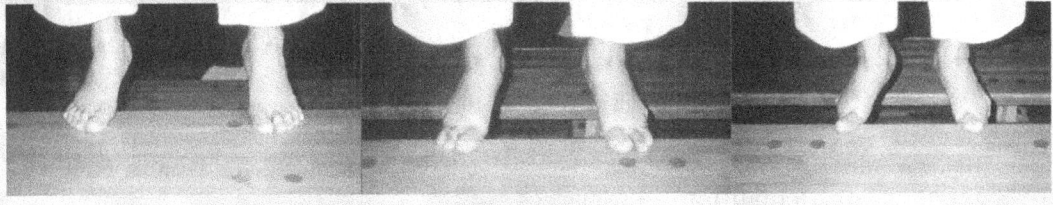

4. Practice holding the toes in the proper striking position. The second toe should be placed over the big toe and the third toe, forming a tight wedge.

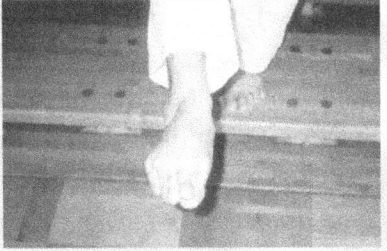

5. Bend the toes backwards. First one foot, then both feet at the same time. When the practitioner masters this exercise, he should start to bounce lightly up and down on his toes while they are bent backwards. After a while, the practitioner should bounce higher

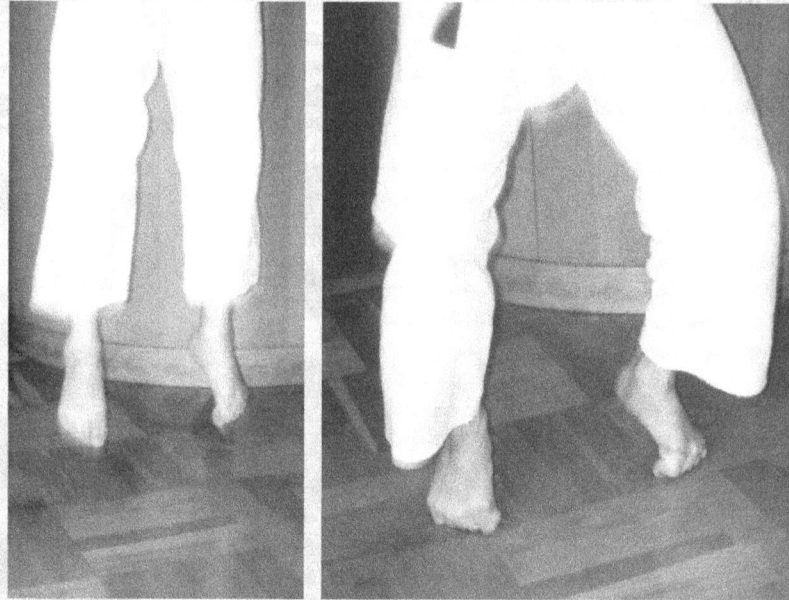

and higher. This exercise is by far the most difficult of all the conditioning exercises.

6. When the practitioner has gained reasonable confidence with the flexibility and strengthening exercises, he should begin to develop striking skills with the toes. Start with a very soft bag and build up to a much harder bag. In Okinawa, practitioners use short makiwara and wooden posts to practice tsumasaki geri.

Chapter 17 — Tsumasaki Geri

Sensei Tajima

18
Kumite

We have explained that kata practice develops "internal timing," whereas kumite practice develops "external timing." Kata practice develops internal timing because, even though the practitioner engages several imaginary opponents, there are never any surprises. The practitioner always knows which direction to face and in what order the imaginary opponents will attack. The objective is to execute the technique properly. Each movement should be done with balance, speed and power. But most of all the practitioner's body mechanics must work in unison to achieve proper internal timing.

In contrast, nothing is certain in kumite. The practitioner must be ready for any and all types of attacks, fakes and combinations. Distance constantly changes and the practitioner must learn to continuously adjust to his opponent. By learning to adapt to constantly changing circumstances, the practitioner develops what Sensei Ota refers to as external timing. Closing the distance, seizing the opening, faking and feinting, and manipulating angles and spatial relationships are all skills requiring external timing. Those skills are developed through kumite training.

Distance vs. Space

Distance from an opponent must be distinguished from the space between the practitioner and the opponent. Distance changes every time either the practitioner or the opponent moves his feet. Space changes every time either the practitioner or the opponent shifts his body. Kumite practice develops the practitioner's ability to manipulate both distance and space, which are both critically important skills for street defense. These skills are not learned through kata practice.

There are practitioners who believe that kumite practice is all that is necessary to gain competence in street fighting. However, according to Sensei Ota, kumite is as far from street fighting as kata is from kumite. Even in free sparring, where neither competitor is bound by pre-determined techniques and responses, the competitiors are bound by specific rules which do not apply to street situations. Most counterattacks, designed to target specific areas of the body in kata training, cannot be used in kumite practice. These kata target zones are almost always considered to be illegal strikes because of the inherent danger to the practitioner. Yet, for self-defense, these responses might be the only way to repel an attacker.

Sensei Ota emphasizes that practicing kumite alone is not sufficient to develop proficiency in street fighting. If the practitioner wishes to learn street fighting, different kinds of training are required, in addition to kumite practice. Sensei Ota has never discouraged his students from endeavoring to train for street defense, yet he vehemently expounds that this is not the primary purpose of Karate-do.

Shigeru Egami in *The Heart of Karate-do* asserts:

> "Sparring was originally a method of practice, not one to decide victory or defeat. It was practiced only to confirm whether a strike or block was effective or not. Although karate is a combat tech-

nique, sparring was not for actual combat nor was it a contest."

Grandmaster Nagamine in *Essence of Okinawan Karate-Do* warns:

"The formal training methods of the great masters of the past must be observed because karate was meant to be pursued as a martial art, not a sport where the goal is defeating an opponent or winning points. Karate has an ancient heritage, full of wisdom. Let us follow the way of karate as shown to us by the masters."

Master Nakayama, Chief Instructor of the Japan Karate Association, writes in *Best Karate: Kumite 1*:

"The man who begins kumite prematurely — without having practiced fundamentals sufficiently — will soon be overtaken by the man who has trained in the basics long and diligently. It is quite simply, a matter of haste makes waste."

Master Nakayama also adds:

"If karate is practiced solely as a fighting technique, this is cause for regret. The fundamental techniques have been developed and perfected through long years of study and practice, but to make any effective use of these techniques, the spiritual aspect of this art of self-defense must be recognized and must play the predominent role."

Sensei Ota continually reminds students that the emphasis for self-defense is developing a strong and flexible body to deliver fast and powerful techniques. The process of doing this creates a strong spirit. But, the true purpose of Karate-do is to develop precision and control. This fosters mental control and discipline, which in turn develops character.

Pre-arranged Sparring

Pre-arranged sparring, or one-step sparring, is the most basic kind of kumite. In this type of practice, one practitioner is designated to attack while the other defends. The particular attack and defense scenarios are pre-determined. The only uncertainty for the defender is the speed and penetration of the attacker's techniques. Pre-arranged sparring, then, teaches the defender to adjust to distance and spacial relationships. It also begins to develop the defender's reaction time, and perhaps most importantly, how to make effective counterattacks.

Semi-free Sparring

Semi-free sparring practice is the next step in kumite training. In this form of training, one practitioner may attack in any way, and the other can defend in any way, using all forms of defense strategies and counterattacks. The offensive and defensive roles are pre-arranged, but the defender does not know how the attacker will attack, nor does the attacker know how the defender will respond. This heightens the intensity of the encounter for both practitioners and helps to develop quick reaction time because there is greater uncertainty with which the defender must contend. There is also an increasing amount of difficulty in counterattacking as well because of the greater amount of surprise. Finally, this type of kumite practice helps the attacker to develop combinations and fakes to create openings in the opponent's defense.

Free Sparring

Free sparring is the ultimate type of kumite practice. In this kind of training, either competitor can attack at any time. There is no predetermined response or counterattack scenarios. Both practitioners can attack or defend and counter without warning. Combinations and fakes are critical for success in free sparring. This ultimately forces practitioners to develop external timing, as well as a better understanding of distance.

Free sparring clearly develops similar skills for street defense. Yet, demonstrating control is critical during practice sessions. As mentioned above, each practitioner is bound by an unspoken set of rules which do not exist on the street. Kata training teaches the practitioner to be prepared for multiple attackers. Kumite practice does not. This is a critical difference between street fighting and free sparring.

All of Sensei Ota's training techniques are geared for real life practical application. Function must take precedent over form. This means that there are right ways to do things and wrong ways. The right ways work; the wrong ways don't. There may be more than one way to execute a move effectively. But until techniques are proven to be effective in real combat situations, they are merely for show. Kumite is a testing ground which helps practioners to find out what works and what doesn't. According to Sensei Ota, this is perhaps the reason why many practitioners feel only kumite is necessary for street defense. Yet, Sensei Ota reminds us that kumite is not the final testing ground. Sensei Ota asserts, "It is true that practitioners should learn to use their weapons, but in learning to control their weapons the practitioner learns Karate-do."

Recognizing the Opening

An opening in kumite refers to the moment when one or both of the practitioners is vulnerable to attack. Openings can occur as a result of either a physical or mental lapse or mistake. Mental openings can only be avoided with diligence and discipline. According to Sensei Ota, practitioners develop mentally when they are taken to the point of exhaustion, yet are encouraged to keep working hard. Physical openings, however, can be avoided by developing a better overall understanding of karate fundamentals. Therefore, the remainder of this chapter focuses on recognizing the openings in an opponent's defense and limiting our own vulnerabilities.

In kumite, the body must function like a spring. When the spring is coiled or squeezed, the practitioner is strong. When the body is uncoiled, the practitioner is weak. Students must learn to recognize when the opponent is uncoiled, because at these moments the opponent does not have enough potential power to do serious damage. Therefore, this opening is the opportune moment to try to break down an opponent's defenses. Students must also learn to recognize when the opponent is coiled, because that is when the oponent is least vulnerable to attack.

To avoid making yourself vulnerable by giving the opponent an opening, footwork is critical. Practitioners are most vulnerable in between movements because there is no tension built up in their stances. Retaining constant tension in the legs while executing combinations is important when the practitioner is attacking. When faking, if the practitioner releases this body tension, generally the fakes will not be convincing.

Closing the Distance

Sensei Ota teaches students that there are two distances of engagement between the praticioner and an opponent. The first is a very close distance in which both opponents are close enough to strike the other with certainty. In a fight, possessing Ikken Hisatsu, or deadly stopping power, makes this short distance a very dangerous range for both opponents. Practitioners that have devoted many years of practice to develop Ikken Hisatsu do not have to concern themselves as much with footwork and fakes. Fakes or feints simply do not apply at this short distance. Ki (chi in Chinese) power and kime (focus) are far more critical in determining the outcome.

At a farther distance, however, footwork and fakes are far more important because they determine which practitioner will be able to close the distance and put himself in a better

Chapter 18 — Kumite

position to finish the fight. Kata concentrates primarily on short distances, even though advanced forms deal with combinations. However, practitioners who do not learn engagement strategies for longer distances and how to close the distance will never be strong at kumite.

Forcing the Opening

To be effective at kumite, the practitioner must acquire expertise at faking strategies because the only way to force an opening at longer distances is with fakes. The first way to use fakes is when attacking. Typically, most practitioners only use fakes in this way. That is, when closing the distance with combination techniques. Generally, the opponent blocks the first attack or fake and gets hit with the second or third technique, which is the real attack. Remember that maintaining body tension when faking is the only way to guarantee that the fakes will be convincing. Sensei Ota demonstrates a simple example:

Correct

Incorrect

1a 1b 1c

2a 2b 2c

263

In this example (1a-1c) Sensei Ota fakes with a front kick to make the opponent react to his kick. Then he delivers a straight punch to the face. In the second example, Ota demonsrates the incorrect technique by not maintaining the tension in his body. Rather, he leans backwards, causing the body to lose the potential power that is necessary to deliver the following strike. Many practitioners make this mistake on the first kick. In this case, the front kick is not convincing because the opponent can back up and get out of range for the subsequent punch to the face. In contrast, in the first example, Sensei Ota maintains tension in the body, which forces the opponent to react to the front kick. It is difficult to move back, because the fake is far more convincing. The opponent can feel that the spring is coiled and must react by attempting to block. This opens up the face for the ensuing straight punch.

Despite the above illustration which uses a front kick as a fake, Sensei Ota cautions students that kicks are easily telegraphed techniques and generally should be reserved for counterattacks only. Most experienced practitioners are generally not faked by a kick. Therefore, practitioners who use kicks to force an opening may put themselves in even worse danger.

The second, and far more subtle and sophisticated way to use fakes, is to draw the opponent in to the practitioner's range. The practitioner must maintain body tension or he will not be able to react quickly enough to the opening in the opponent's defense. Sensei Ota demonstrates this principle below:

1

2

3

In this sequence, Sensei Ota draws the opponent towards himself by pulling his own front foot in, causing the opponent to believe that he is off guard and thus open to attack. In fact, Sensei Ota keeps the spring coiled by keeping the tension in his legs when he steps back. The left arm works like a counter weight to improve balance. When the opponent moves in, Sensei Ota simultaneously strikes with the opposite arm. To make the opponent move in, the practitioner must have an impeccable sense of distance and timing.

Counterattacks

To counterattack effectively, the practitioner must always maintain tension in the legs. The direction or angle the practitioner moves in is not the issue. Rather, the distance must always be close enough to effectively come back to counterattack. If the practitioner moves out of range, he is simply running away to avoid attack. This is not, however, good karate technique. Students should begin with pre-arranged sparring drills to gain a better understanding of distance and then move to free sparring to better test what they have learned in pre-arranged sparring practice. Keep in mind that it becomes increasingly more difficult for the practitioner to get into the proper position to counterattack when the opponent is able to use fakes.

Section Four
KOBUDO

19
Kobudo

In the year 1609, the Lord of the Satsuma clan sent an army of Japanese samurai to conquer and subjugate the people of the Ryukyu Islands, including the tiny island of Okinawa. Prior to then, Okinawan bushi had learned swordsmanship and related arts from the Japanese. Even the sai was a favored weapon of Samurai from the Kyushu region of Japan, before it came to be used in Okinawan kobudo. After 1609, all metal swords and spears were confiscated and their use was forbidden.

In *Unante: The Secrets of Karate*, John Sells, the noted historian and karate and kobudo instructor, articulates:

> "If perchance any of the old Okinawan Bushi were forced to defend themselves, they did so without the use of the sword or spear. However, Okinawan Bushi were not likely to face personal combat armed with only their bare hands if they could do otherwise. Therefore, the Okinawan people developed fighting techniques using farming and fishing equipment, the only possible weapons not taken away by the Japanese."

John Sells continues to point out when fighting with weapons: "It is the rare man who could defend himself against an armed Samurai warrior. Most probably, this simply was not done, and if it was, it was certainly the exception to the rule."

Nowadays, karate is one of the most widely practiced martial arts in the world, with millions of practitioners from dozens of different styles and organizations around the world. Kobudo, by comparison, is a rarefied art form limited to but a handful of practitioners. The number of surviving sensei is even smaller. As a consequence, the vast majority of  karate schools do not teach kobudo as part of their regular curriculum. This, however, represents a major departure from the original traditions of Okinawan martial arts. According to Shinken Gima, tenth- degree black belt and master of Shotokan karate who demonstrated alongside Gichin Funakoshi at the Kodokan, said that, "In the old days, bushi practiced kobudo more than karate."

John Sells writes in *Unante: The Secrets of Karate*:

"What we do know of the history of kobudo is a fascinating story that compliments and enlightens our knowledge of karate overall. For in truth, karate and kobudo should not be seen as separate arts, but as a single inter-related martial method."

The origins of the modern day popularization of karate trace back to its adoption as a form of physical education in the

Okinawan public school system. That change was initiated by the legendary karate master, Anko Itosu. Before then, martial arts in Okinawa were practiced primarily in secret, as they had been for centuries, out of fear of being discovered by the imperialistic Japanese. In part, Anko Itosu's success was due to his emphasis on the study of Karate-do (the way of karate), which fosters the development of character and spirit, as opposed to Karate-jutsu (the martial application of karate), which is strictly for combat. Kobudo did not fit the curriculum for public schools because of the perception that weapons are inherently too violent. Ever since then, the emphasis of karate training has steadily drifted away from the traditional origins of the art practiced by the ancient bushi to a more popular form of physical training and recreation that is better adapted to modern life. An unfortunate and unintentional result is that the ancient art of kobudo has become increasingly obscured. Today kobudo is rarely practiced, even among karate devotees.

According to Sensei Ota, there are three primary reasons why karate students should practice kobudo. The first reason is that kobudo training strengthens the muscles of the body: hands, fingers, arms, shoulders and especially hips, in ways that ordinary karate training cannot achieve. Kobudo training helps practitioners to make dramatic breakthroughs in their empty-hand technique in a remarkably short period of time. Kobudo develops greater understanding of body mechanics and distance, which are critical concepts for karate practitioners. Historically, Ikken Hisatsu, or one-punch stopping power, was the ultimate goal of karate training in Okinawa. According to Sensei Ota, kobudo training is indispensable in the development of Ikken Hisatsu. Therefore, this makes kobudo training fundamental to the development of karate.

The second reason, and perhaps even more important than the physical attributes gained through weapons practice, is the mental preparation and awareness which is honed by kobudo practice. Because of the inherent danger in training with weapons, kobudo forces the practitioner to exercise the highest level of concentration and focus. This may ultimately be the most important skill a warrior can possess. Sensei Ota believes that if students do not train in kobudo, their training will not fully prepare them either mentally or physically for anything beyond point fighting competitions.

Sensei Ota at Shuri Castle, which is in Okinawa.

The third reason that kobudo training is an important supplement to karate training is that it allows practitioners from all the different styles of martial arts to train together. Empty-hand fighting techniques can vary dramatically between different styles, often with distinctive variations. In contrast, kobudo techniques transcend stylistic boundaries. Sensei Ota explains that training with practitioners from different styles promotes the exchange of knowledge and ideas. This helps to develop an even greater understanding of body mechanics and distance, which are critical in karate.

In Okinawa, practitioners from different schools frequently train together. Nevertheless, outside Okinawa, and particularly between Japanese stylists, training rarely crosses over stylistic boundaries. This only leads to political disputes and closed-minded thinking. To Sensei Ota, kobudo offers the best solution because everyone can practice kobudo together and still derive a mutual benefit.

KOBUDO FUNDAMENTALS

Stances

The stances used when wielding weapons are exactly the same as the stances used in empty-hand traditions. Practitioners must learn to shift from one stance to another, to move in and out, change distance and change angles just as in karate. Because the stances used in kobudo and karate are the same, so are the body mechanics. Therefore, training in one helps to develop the other. (Please refer to the section on kata for a more technical discussion of stances).

Blocks

Sensei Ota explains that blocking with weapons is like catching a baseball. Good fielders are sometimes described as having "soft hands." When good fielders catch a baseball, they pull their gloves back slightly when receiving the ball. This helps to absorb the force of the impact and ensures that the baseball does not pop out of their glove. Blocking is exactly the same, and nowhere is this illustrated more clearly than in kobudo.

According to Sensei Ota, when executing a block with a weapon, it is critical to receive the opponent's weapon with soft hands, rather than banging against another object with your weapon. In this way, the kobudo practitioner can re-direct an opponent's attack. The same way that a fielder pulls the glove when catching a baseball, the kobudo practitioner must develop soft blocks. Sensei Ota asserts that this is done by bending the knees and dropping the weight in his stances. That is, a successful block is achieved with the body, not the weapon. Just like with empty hands, blocking should not be done by clashing power against power. Rather it is a matter of reducing the opponent's power while the practitioner controls his own body movements.

Regardless of the type of weapon, the kobudo practitioner must make the weapon an extension of his body. It is very important, according to Sensei Ota, that kobudo practitioners do not reach to make blocks. It is better to keep the weapon close to the body. Indeed, this is also a fundamental principle in empty-handed karate techniques as well.

Stopping the Weapon

If a practitioner of karate does not have control of his body movements, he is vulnerable to attack from an opponent. However, the outcome may not be fatal. Indeed, in many styles of karate, especially Naha-te styles, practitioners train to endure blows from the opponent and still continue to fight. With kobudo, however, there is no margin for error. Achieving control of a weapon requires the skill to stop the weapon as well as to swing it with power and accuracy. When the practitioner swings his weapon, it is crucial that he can bring the weapon to a complete stop as quickly as possible. This is absolutely critical for combinations, because otherwise the practitioner will not be able to set up for the next move quickly enough. To Sensei Ota, combinations in kobudo are equally as important as they are in empty hand situations.

Kata

Sensei Ota argues that, unlike karate, it is not necessary to know a large number of kobudo forms. Developing proficiency at a small number of kata is more than sufficient to gain a deep understanding of a given weapon. Moreover, Sensei Ota recommends learning kata from different styles, especially with the bo. This is because different kobudo styles emphasize different swings and blocks. Therefore, knowing kobudo kata from only one system is too limiting.

20
Kama

Consistent with most Okinawan karate and kobudo instructors throughout history, Sensei Ota believes that martial arts is a private pursuit an individual must follow largely alone, often in secret. Knowledge is passed on selectively, sometimes only to a chosen few. Gaining publicity for one's skill is better left to entertainers. But that characteristic modesty also has kept the true karate and kobudo adepts out of the public spotlight. Therefore, their knowledge is sometimes very difficult to acquire, if not impossible.

It is difficult to describe Sensei Ota's ability with the kama. The best way is to recall that classic martial arts film, *Enter the Dragon,* in which Bruce Lee is swinging the nunchaku. Then, imagine adding razor-sharp blades to the ends of the sticks, and accelerating the speed to the point that the blades whiz by so fast that they are almost imperceptible. Bruce

Lee's demonstration with the nunchaku is good entertainment, but the sense of danger one feels from watching Sensei Ota perform with the kama is truly awesome. Even the most experienced and discriminating practitioners are awed by his impressive control with such a deadly weapon.

The History

The military subjugation by Japan forced Okinawa's aristocrats to devise new methods of protecting themselves, their families and villages. By applying their knowledge of fighting arts, they adapted common farming and fishing implements for self-defense purposes. The result was that those weapons, adapted by the Okinawans from utilitarian tools, have become important weapons for kobudo practitioners, and styles have developed around each of the types of weapons they used.

Ni-cho Kamajutsu means using a pair of common garden sickles, or kama, in a martial way. The kama, perhaps more than any other weapon, traces its origins back to farming. A bladed weapon, the kama is a genuine farmer's tool that has been used for centuries by farmers in Okinawa and Japan. The origin of the kama as a farming implement is well documented. Grandmaster Nagamine writes in *The Essence of Okinawan Karate-Do*, "The kama, a hand sickle, is still widely used as a farming implement in Okinawa today." Indeed, the best quality kama can be purchased at ordinary hardware and garden supply stores in Okinawa. These kama are produced for farmers and intended for actual labor in the fields. They look and feel very different than the flashy kama often used by practitioners in tournament competitions.

Choosing a Weapon

Sensei Ota explains to students that it is not necessary to become proficient in all of the traditional kobudo weapons. Rather, for battle it is important to practice and master only one weapon. After all, Sensei Ota asserts, "In combat it is only possible to use one weapon at a time, and it ought to be the one you are the most comfortable with."

Sensei Ota recommends choosing a weapon based upon an emotional response: "Because that weapon calls out to you." Ever since Sensei Ota began learning the kama it has been special to him. Undoubtedly, the inherent danger in handling the kama was an attractive feature to a man like Ota, who prides himself not on his ability to generate lethal force, but also, and perhaps more importantly, on his ability to control it!

The risks involved in kama training may be the primary reason why it is less commonly practiced than other traditional Okinawan weapons. Practitioners should heed Grandmaster Nagamine's warning: "Insufficient practice may result in self-inflicted injury." While bumps and bruises are a customary part of kobudo training, no other weapon is as dangerous to the practitioners themselves as the kama. Sensei Ota recalls many instances in which new students of the kama seriously wounded themselves and even severed their own fingers. Ota himself bears many scars from the kama. One time he lodged the kama point so deeply into his shin bone that the blade bent and a piece of the tip chipped off when he removed it from his leg.

For this reason, when Ota came to the United States he used to recommend the kama only for people who were mentally ready to confront life-and-death situations. However, over the years, he has changed his mind and now believes that practicing the kama is beneficial because it forces students to concentrate and focus. In this way, kama training helps both kobudo and karate students to develop mental discipline.

Comparisons between different kobudo weapons are frequently made by both karate and kobudo stylists. Yet, Sensei

Ota firmly believes that practitioners should not compare one weapon to another. Each weapon has its own advantages and disadvantages. Any weapon is potentially deadly when wielded by an expert. However, the kama, because of the sharpness of the blades, more than any other weapon, demands the highest level of focus and concentration to practice. In Sensei Ota's kobudo classes, he prefers to see students develop reasonable proficiency in at least one or two other weapons before beginning to train with the kama.

Ota's Background with the Kama

The first time Sensei Ota tried the kama was with Master Chokei Kishaba, a contemporary of Master Masao Shima. Master Kishaba is the older brother of Chogi Kishaba, the headmaster of Yamane-ryu kobudo. Master Kishaba is one of the most expert kobudo practitioners in Shorin-ryu. He, in turn, learned the kama from the legendary, Grandmaster Hohan Soken (1889–1983). Master Kishaba began studying all the kobudo weapons from Grandmaster Soken when he was in his late twenties. Although Ota, like Kishaba, is proficient in all of the major Okinawan kobudo weapons, they both prefer the bo and kama.

Remembering his early days of study with Master Kishaba, Ota has said:

> "Kishaba would come to the Shima dojo to teach us kobudo. But he didn't want to teach kama at the school. One day, he suggested that anyone who wanted to learn kama should come to his house. A group of us, maybe nine or 10, went over to his house, and we just talked about karate and the meaning of the martial arts. Kishaba had some very old Chinese books about martial arts, which he showed us. Finally he got out the kama and gave them to us to look at and feel. He

wanted us to get a general idea of what the weapon was, so that it could make an impression on us before we tried to use it. Then a few of us began trying the basic motions, with only one kama. A basic downward swing, a horizontal swing, a diagonal swing, all just with one kama, in a natural stance, the other arm at the side out of the way."

Sensei Ota explains that it is important to start in a natural stance because it reduces the chance of slicing the legs and knees.

Kishaba went on to instruct Sensei Ota in the basic combative principles of Ni-cho Kamajutsu. After learning the basics with one arm, the next thing that practitioners need to develop, according to Master Kishaba, was the coordination to simultaneously move the kama around the body in a synchronized fashion from one position to another without causing bodily injury to themselves. This is a great deal more difficult than it sounds.

Sensei Ota's other kama teacher was Mr. Kinjo. While Mr. Kinjo is not widely known in karate circles outside Okinawa, he is both respected and feared for his powerful position as an influential businessman and ties to the Japanese mainland. Sensei Ota recalls that Mr. Kinjo trained frequently at the Shima dojo. Like Sensei Ota, Mr. Kinjo was attracted to the rough sparring sessions at the Shima dojo, rather than the more classical kata training methods preferred at Grandmaster Nagamine's honbu.

Mr. Kinjo is responsible for teaching Sensei Ota how to attach a rope to the end of one kama and swing it around the body. This technique is most probably a Japanese innovation that derived from the kusarigama. Most Okinawan stylists do not swing the kama, but grip the weapon firmly for blocking and striking. According to Sensei Ota, the swinging motion is used to extend the distance and to keep an opponent at a safe distance. When fighting multiple opponents, the swinging technique is extremely useful.

SWINGING THE KAMA

The kama can be swung in either a vertical motion, over the shoulder, or in a horizontal motion, around the back. Some stylists will attach both kama to a rope and swing them around the body. This, however, has no practical value for fighting. According to Sensei Ota, swinging the kama can be risky because it is harder to maintain control of the weapon. Learning to tightly grasp the kama after it has been swung requires diligent practice and is a technique that should only be learned after the basic techniques of blocking, hooking and striking are mastered.

Vertical Swing

When executing a vertical swing, the arm generally starts in an upright angle with the sickle held above shoulder height. The kama is thrown forward while pointing the tip of the blade at the desired target. If the weapon doesn't strike the opponent, it swings in a downward arc and the rope wraps around the hand one to two times and is then re-grasped. From this position, the kama can be swung in a backwards arc... that is in a

reverse motion from the first swing. But on the reverse swing it is the first two inches of the top of the blade that is aimed upwards at the opponent, instead of downward at the opponent as in the forward swing.

Horizontal Swing

When executing the horizontal swing, the blade of the kama is turned sideways by bending the wrist and the blade is launched with the tip of the kama aimed at the opponent. On this swing, the weapon moves around the body and is stopped by the practitioner's own body. Sensei Ota explains that until the partitioner can master how far to move his arm, given the length of the rope, students will frequently cut the sides, hips and back of their bodies. The ideal place to stop the kama is in the middle of the back. If the arm is extended too far, the kama swings around and can cut the opposite hip area. If the arm is not extended far enough, the kama may cut the other hip. To reduce the amount of injury, Sensei Ota recommends that students wrap the blades with masking tape when they are first learning. Some practitioners use wooden kama to reduce the risk of injury. Sensei Ota advises against that because the weight and feel of wooden kama are dramatically different than

the real weapons; therefore, it ultimately does not serve to reduce injury if and when these students switch to using real blades.

An expert with the kama should be able to skillfully manipulate the weapon blindfolded, as if it were merely an extension of his own body. Sensei Ota started training with the kama in front of the mirror, with plenty of light. Then he eventually progressed to the point that he could practice in total darkness. This is the only way, Sensei Ota explains, that a person can be intimately familiar with his weapon. The length of the rope used for swinging motions is a matter of individual preference. A longer rope results in greater distance, but Sensei Ota believes that the rope should only be long enough to wrap around the hand one or two times. Any longer, he argues, makes it easier for the opponent to catch the kama in flight during the arc of its swing.

Chapter 20 — Kama

BASIC APPLICATIONS

The wooden portion of the shaft between the grip and the blade is used for blocking. The curved shape of the blade makes it ideal for hooking and pulling techniques. Sensei Ota explains that only the first two inches or so of the blade is used for striking or cutting, especially when swinging the kama. The rope should be bound around the bottom of the shaft to make for a surer grip.

The basic combative principles of Ni-cho Kamajutsu, according to Sensei Ota, are similar to karate basics both from a standpoint of strategy and application. In the first photograph of the sequence on page 286, Sensei Ota demonstrates one of the basic empty-hand blocks; the second photograph shows an effective counterattack; the third photograph demonstrates the same block using the kama (the hooking motion follows as part of the blocking technique); the fourth photograph demonstrates a counterattack with the kama; the fifth and sixth photographs show the same block-and-counter sequence with the tonfa.

Outside Block

Kuro-Matsu No [Kuro] Kama

Translated into English, Kuro-Matsu, [means "black pine] tree." Sensei Ota has chosen to select this [name for the] kata he created. The "Matsu" character in J[apanese is the same] ideogram used in the name Matsubayashi[-ryu. Sensei Ota is] recognized as one of the world's leading ade[pts of this style, and] he has chosen to name this form in memo[ry of the late] Shoshin Nagamine, the founder of Matsub[ayashi-ryu. In this] way, Ota hopes, the Matsubayashi-ryu nam[e will remain in the] minds of the younger generation of practiti[oners.]

Sensei Ota specially wanted to design a k[ata suitable for] tournament competitions. Even though he [is one of the lead-]ing experts on swinging the kama on a rope[, he feels that this] is far too dangerous for most competitors[, and most kama] experts do not possess the dedication to lea[rn to swing this] weapon on the end of a rope. For this r[eason, Ota has not] included that type of swinging techniques [in this kata for] Ni-cho kama.

Sensei Ota at Grandmaster Nagamine['s grave]

Lower Block

Rising Block

EMPTY HAND

KAMA

TONFA

The World Tournament, celebrating Okinawan karate and kobudo that is held biannually in Naha, only allows competitors to choose from a pre-selected series of bo and sai kata. Sensei Ota feels this is short sighted. Certainly, tonfa or kama or nunchaku are as legitimate a choice of a weapon as the bo or sai. Perhaps the problem is that the kata for these other weapons are relatively obscure or cannot be traced back to specific lineages. Yet, to Sensei Ota, this does not mean that other weapons should not be allowed in the competitions. Sensei Ota hopes some day this will change. When it does, there will have to be established kata on which to judge the competitors. Sensei Ota hopes some day Kuro-Matsu No Ni-Cho Kama will be accepted as an official kata for tournaments, including the World Tournament in Naha.

1 *2* *3* *4*

Chapter 20 — Kama

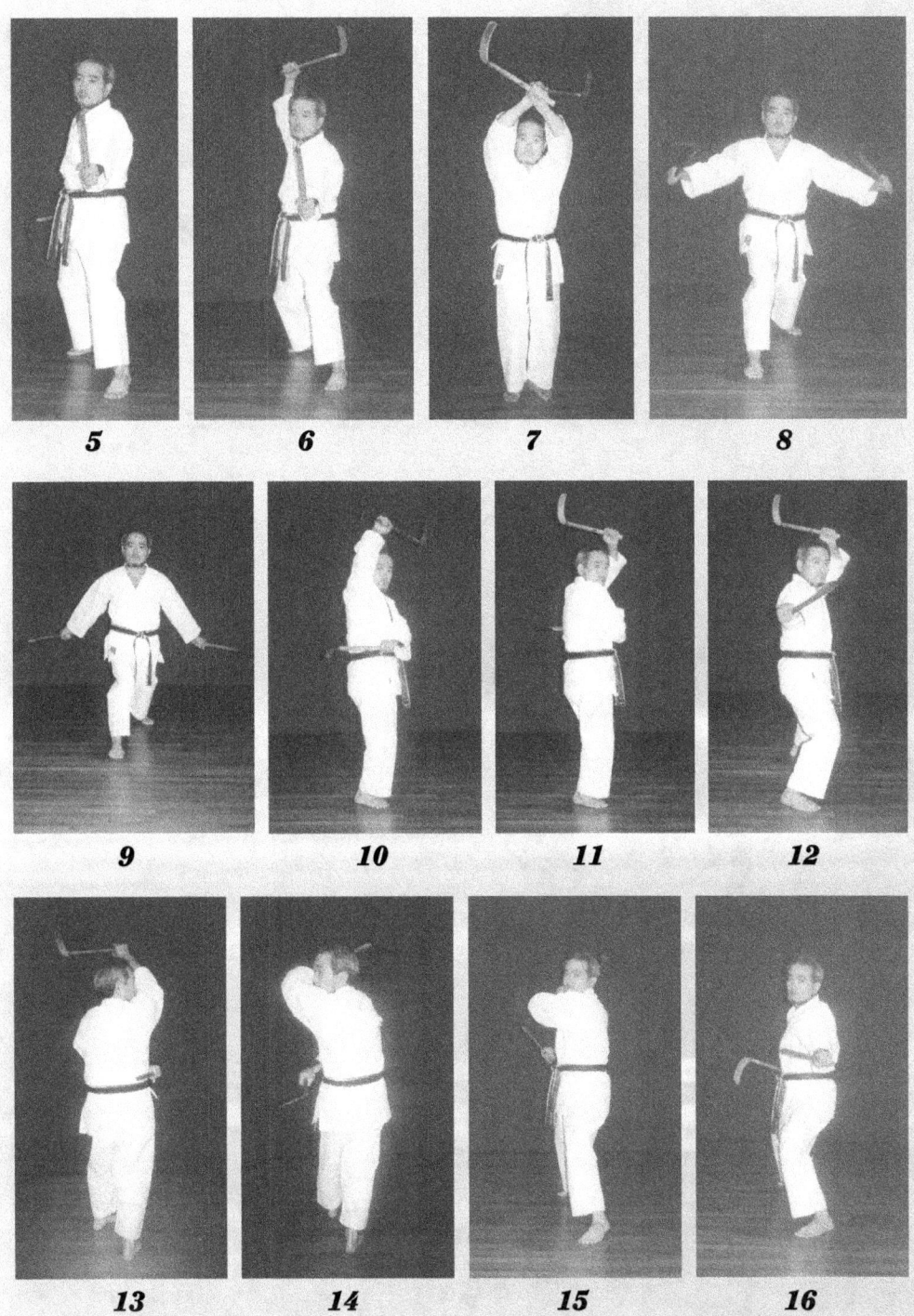

291

Okinawan Karate

Chapter 20 — Kama

293

Okinawan Karate

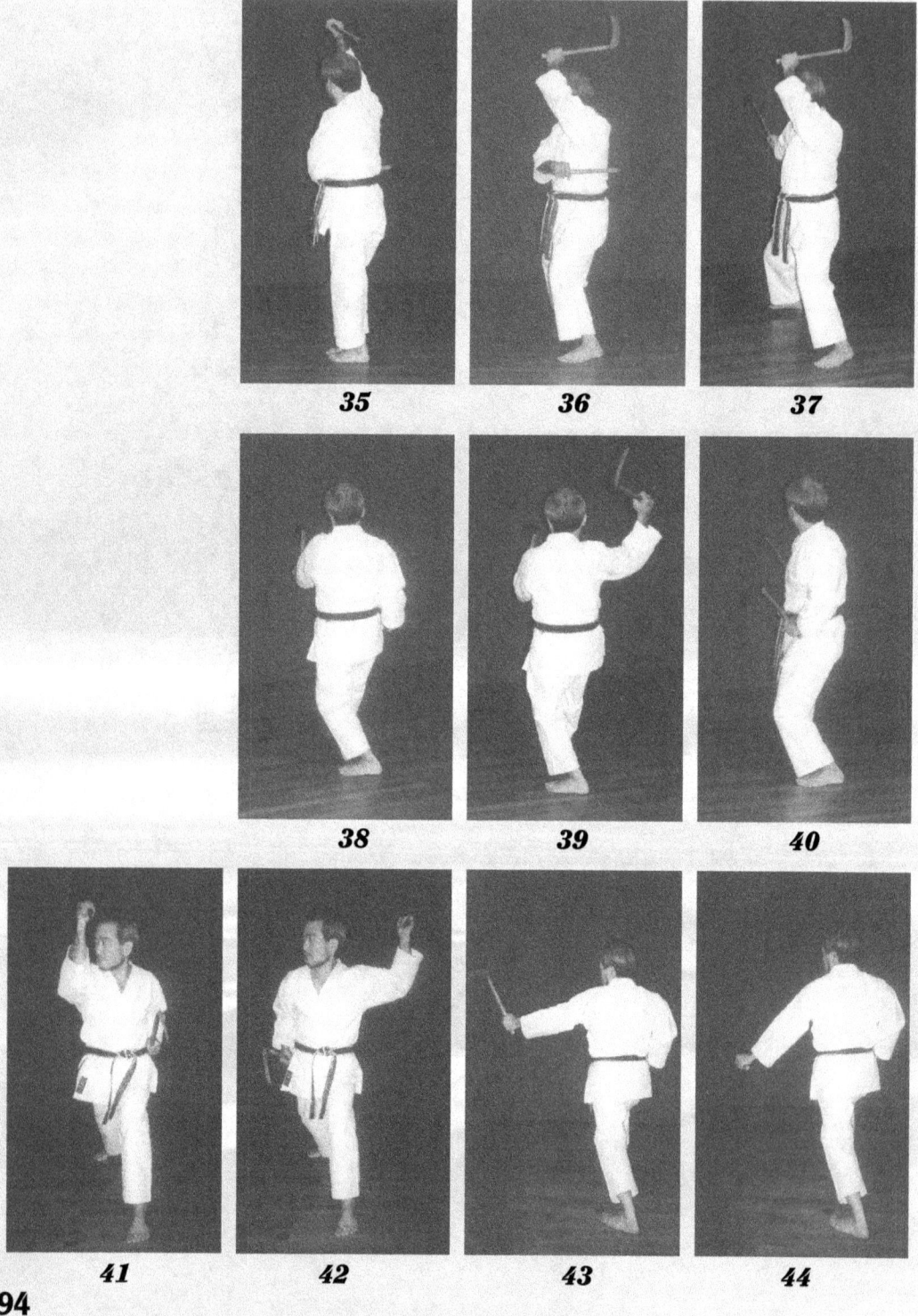

294

Chapter 20 — Kama

45 *46* *47*

48 *49* *50*

51 *52* *53*

295

Okinawan Karate

Chapter 20 — Kama

62   *63*   *64*   *65*

21
Bo

The bo is the most widely used weapon in Okinawan kobudo. Sensei Ota believes that the bo is the most effective weapon because of its long reach. It is extremely unlikely that Okinawan bushi, armed with kobudo weapons only, were able to defeat Japanese samurai armed with swords. However, with the bo it is possible to defeat even a sword, due to the longer reach of the staff. To Sensei Ota, the reach of the bo makes it the most desirable weapon for battle, even more than sai or kama, which also can inflict deadly harm. This is even more evident, according to Sensei Ota, when the practitioner faces multiple opponents.

Karate styles are defined by kata. However, with the bo, style is defined by the way that the weapon is used and manipulated. Amongst the most popular traditions of bojutsu are the Matayoshi and Yabiku-Taira styles. Recently, much attention has been focused on Yamane-ryu bojutsu and its unique footwork and mechanics.

Okinawan Karate

Regardless of the style one practices, Sensei Ota suggests that it is not necessary to learn more than a handful of forms. Learning a greater number is redundant. Moreover, bojutsu practitioners can apply the principles and mechanics of one style to another without having to learn more kata. It is more important to learn to swing the bo effectively and to learn to control the weapon than to learn many kata.

Forward Swing

The forward swing can be done with either foot forward, just like punching in karate. The body mechanics differ slightly, just as they are different between the lunge punch and the reverse punch. The goal is to generate maximum speed and power without losing control. Controlling the weapon and coming to a complete stop is critical because it sets up the next move, just like setting up combinations in karate. The bo is stopped either under the arm or over the arm depending on the technique or the style. In combat situations, circumstances dictate whether one method or another is required.

Forward Swing (Lunge)

1

2

3

4

Chapter 21 — Bo

Forward Swing (Reverse)

1

2

3

4

Sensei Ota says that it is important to learn kata from different bojutsu styles. The following example above demonstrates the basic swing of Yamane-ryu. The bo swings in a near vertical arc and the practitioner stops the weapon under his arm against the body. However, if the angle of the swing is more horizontal (i.e. a head-level attack) than vertical, the bo can only be controlled by stopping the weapon over the arm. This is the basic swing used most often in the Matayoshi-ryu. Both swings are important. If the bojutsu practitioner does not learn both, and more importantly, if he does not learn to stop the weapon using both techniques, his ability to defend himself with the staff is severely diminished.

Matayoshi-ryu

Yamane-ryu

Back Sweep

Although the back sweep is an uncommon technique in most bo kata, it is nevertheless one of the most effective techniques for battle. The reason, Sensei Ota argues, is that the opponent cannot read where the bo is going to attack. The bo practitioner can attack the knees or the face without revealing his intentions until the very last moment. It is an effective swing because the practitioner can easily surprise his opponent. It is also one of the most powerful swings. Moreover, the back sweep is an excellent strike in counterattack situations.

Back Sweep

1 *2* *3* *4*

When executing the back sweep, rotate the hips fully and twist the upper body. Try not to generate power on the swing from swinging the weapon, but from twisting the body. Keep the bo close to the body to increase the speed of the swing. Control the body by stopping it against the shoulder.

Reverse Swing

The bo practitioner should first prepare by twisting his body to increase tension in the joints, then uncoil the body and time this with the swing of the staff.

The hands turn over and the weapon is stopped by the back of the rib cage. This technique is common in Yamane-ryu bo kata and is also extremely effective when counterattacking.

Reverse Swing

1 2 3

Thrust

There are two ways to execute a forward thrust with the bo. The first type of thrust is made with the arms; the hands do not move. The second type of thrust requires the practitioner to move his hands along the weapon. In this thrust, both hands rotate inwards, or towards each other. The lead hand grips the bo lightly and the rear hand slides the weapon, similar to using a pool cue to strike a pool ball, except that the rear hand also twists as the hand thrusts.

Thrust (#1)

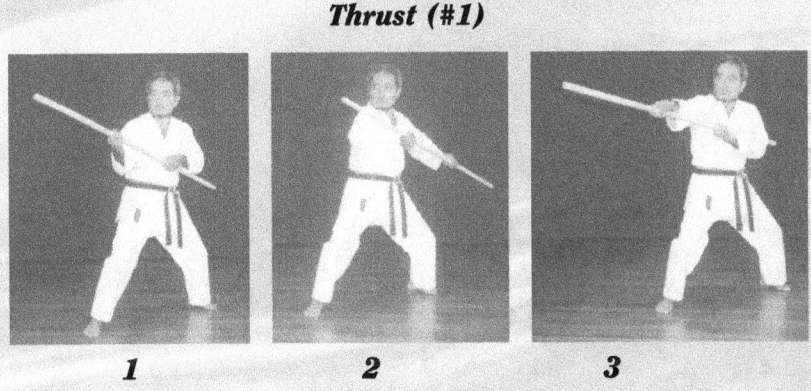

1 2 3

Okinawan Karate

Thrust (#2)

1 2 3

Poke

Pokes are used to attack specific areas of an opponent's body by using the end of the bo. As with the second type of thrust, one hand slides the weapon and the other hand guides the weapon. The difference is in the retraction. Unlike a thrust, which is left extended, a poke is retracted immediately after it is extended. Sensei Ota is pictured executing a commonly used poke to the lower parts of the opponent's body. He is also pictured executing a less commonly used poke to the face area of the opponent.

Poke (#1)

Poke (#2)

Chapter 21 — Bo

Blocking

Most practitioners, including many experts, do not understand the proper way to use the bo for blocking. Most videos that demonstrate the bo show the practitioner reaching to block the opponent's weapon with his own bo. To Sensei Ota, this is completely impractical. There is absolutely no possibility of blocking an opponent's attack this way. First, it is impossible to anticipate the attack, and, second, the momentum from the opponent's swing would overwhelm the practitioners block, possibly even breaking the weapon.

According to Sensei Ota, the proper way to use the bo in blocking is to keep the weapon close to the body. Try to cover the body, and "receive" the opponent's swing (just like the idea of "soft hands" in empty-hand blocking techniques). By shifting the feet and maneuvering to gain an advantageous angle, the practitioner can diffuse the power and momentum of the opponent's swing.

Application

Application

This method may appear more risky because the opponent's weapon gets much closer to its target, i.e. the practitioner's own body. However, it is the only way to accurately judge the opponent's attack and respond accordingly. Reaching out to cover the distance will never work in combat situations. Practitioners who use the weapon in that way have not sufficiently considered its potential efficacy in combat situations.

22
Tonfa

Anyone can walk in off the street and buy a traditional Okinawan kobudo weapon. There are many martial arts supply stores and catalogues that provide weapons to kobudo practitioners. However, according to Sensei Ota, these standardized weapons become unsatisfactory once a kobudo practitioner develops more advanced techniques.

Over time practitioners must learn to customize their weapons according to their physique. Ultimately, the weapon must become an extension of the practitioner's body. Sensei Ota has made some very subtle changes to his tonfa, which to the unsophisticated eye are barely perceptible. Yet, these changes have advanced his technique and consequently have taken Sensei Ota to a higher level of skill. However, before a student can run out and make his own customized tonfa, he must first understand the proper way to use the tonfa.

Basic Covering

Sensei Ota is pictured holding the tonfa in the basic blocking positions. These blocks are very similar to the basic blocking techniques in most systems of karate.

Rising Block

Inside Block

Outside Block

Downward Block

The hands and arms should snap into final position at the point of contact in the same way empty-hand blocking techniques should snap. In the illustrations provided, notice that the tonfa fully covers the arm and extends past the elbow. The tonfa is held firmly across the arm much in the same fashion as the bow is held when swinging the weapon across the body. The tonfa is held in this fashion to prevent it from slipping off the arm and thus leaving the arm exposed. Moreover, if the tonfa is not gripped tightly against the arm, it is difficult to control swinging movements and combinations. To better accommodate the way the tonfa rests on the practitioner's forearm, Sensei Ota has made subtle adjustments to the handle of the tonfa to improve the practitioner's control.

Swinging Blocks and Strikes

Over decades of observation, Sensei Ota has found that most tonfa practitioners grip the tonfa loosely in the palm of the hand, allowing the weapon to spin around in an uncontrolled manner. This technique is ineffective for combat and generates very little power or speed. Sensei Ota frequently reminds his students that techniques executed in this manner will result in the practitioner losing his weapon, potentially a mortal error.

Instead, the tonfa must be gripped tightly throughout the swing. The weapon does move slightly in the hand, but it is primarily the whipping of the elbow and wrist in unison that determines the speed and resulting power of the technique.

Sensei Ota is pictured executing several swinging blocks or strikes. Note that the mechanics for blocking techniques are the same for strikes. This is true for the bo and other kobudo weapons as well.

Okinawan Karate

Horizontal Swing

Vertical Swing

Chapter 22 — Tonfa

Diagonal Swing

Outside Snap

311

TONFA DESIGN

The Handle

The shape of the handle needs to be adjusted to the proper length and diameter to fit each practitioner's particular hand size. Without the proper grip, the tonfa cannot be used effectively. If the space between the handle's head and the shaft of the weapon is too short for the practitioner's hand, then it will be difficult to generate enough speed when swinging the tonfa. Conversely, if the space is too large, practitioners will not be able to hold the tonfa tightly enough to generate sufficient force when contact is made. Moreover, it makes it virtually impossible to bring the weapon to a controlled stop at the end of a technique, which results in combinations that appear clumsy and slow.

The placement of the knob at the end of the handle is critical because it determines the actual length of the gripping area. When the grip is squeezed tightly, the muscles in the hand contract and the hand expands, pressing against the knob and creating more friction to stop the movement of the tonfa, like a disc brake in a car. Without the knob, the swinging movement cannot be stopped.

Another important design issue involves the angle at which the handle is set. The handle has to be exactly the correct angle relative to the shaft so that when the return motion is completed the weapon rests firmly against the arm and comes to a complete stop. This adjustment by Sensei Ota may be the most revolutionary development in the history of the tonfa and has allowed him to bring his level of skill far past what others have been able to achieve. Indeed, many tonfa practitioners have commissioned Sensei Ota to personally design tonfa for them with these improvements. Across the board this has resulted in quantum leaps for those practitionerss in terms of both their technique and their understanding of proper tonfa body mechanics.

The Shaft

Sensei Ota cautions practitioners that if they are using the prefabricated weapons like those commercially available, then they may injure themselves if they practice using the proper swinging techniques. To correct for this problem, Sensei Ota carves the inside of the weapon to conform to the shape of the forearm. In this way, the practitioner can swing the tonfa at full power and return to its resting position without banging the tonfa painfully hard against the wrist or forearm, causing bruises and possibly even broken bones.

The proportion of wood on either side of the handle is also critically important. If the front portion of the tonfa is too long relative to the rest of the tonfa, then the weapon will be too heavy to generate enough speed. If the front portion is too short relative to the rest of the tonfa, then the weapon will be too unbalanced to control the technique at the point of impact.

Most experts recommend that the tonfa should extend completely beyond the elbow for protection. Sensei Ota prefers his tonfa to be significantly longer than most practitioners. However, this is largely a matter of personal preference. The longer tonfa is considerably more difficult to control than a shorter tonfa, but Sensei Ota asserts that it increases the speed and resulting power of the technique. This presupposes that the practitioner has developed sufficient control to handle the longer length. Furthermore, the added length provides extra protection when held in the defensive positions.

Kobudo practitioners are commonly seen thrusting the tonfa like a punch with the long portion of the shaft extended. However, with prefabricated tonfa there is not enough wood on the front portion of the shaft, nor does the shape conform to the forearm to sufficiently control the thrust. To correct for this, Sensei Ota has designed the front end of the shaft to be extra long. Moreover, his tonfa is angled to fit the shape of the practitioner's forearm.

Sensei Ota is shown thrusting the tonfa with both the long and short ends of the weapon.

Notice the following points illustrated in the photograph below: 1. Sensei Ota's design (below) is carved away to leave room for the practitioner's wrist and forearm; 2. The angle of the handle 3. The contour of the shaft; 4. The positioning of the handle in relation to the proportion of fore and aft sections of the shaft.

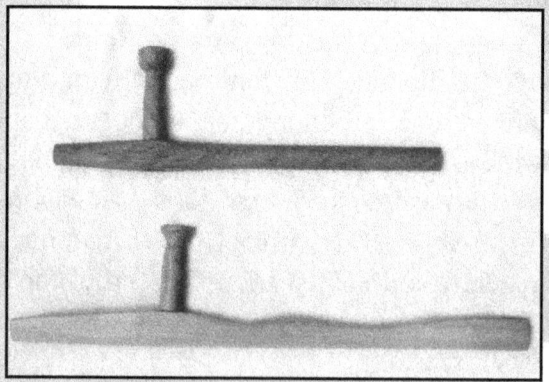

Choice of Wood

Every wood functions differently because weight and density react differently when contact is made. Japanese red oak is the highest quality wood. It is also the most expensive. It is preferred because it is hard and heavy. However, hardwood specialty stores carry far heavier and denser woods than Japanese red oak. These include maple, teak, black walnut and aged ironwood. Sensei Ota is currently experimenting with a variety of these woods. Some woods, like the aged ironwood, may be far too heavy for actual combat, but are very helpful for training and building hand and arm strength. Lighter woods allow students to focus on snapping and swinging techniques and are good for kata competition. For combat, heavier woods are better for covering blocks. Sensei Ota believes it is best to have several tonfa for different types of training and combat situations.

Mark Bishop, in his book *Zen Kobudo*, provides a historical context for the use of different kinds of woods:

> "Materials, such as locally grown tropical hardwoods, which once abounded in the Ryukyu Islands, were favoured, with Yaeyama sendangi (sandalwood, or rosewood, from Iriomote or Ishigaki Island in Yaeyama) being the favourite. Very hard, high quality kuroki (ebony) was also frequently used."

Conclusion

Every once in a great while an extroadinary genius with aptitude for karate and kobudo makes changes to the art that become permanent and help to improve the overall skill of future generations of practitioners. Such is the case with Sensei Ota and his revolutionary designs for the tonfa. Years from now these changes may become the standard for all tonfa. After years of training, Sensei Ota has refined the weapon to enhance his fighting technique. These subtle changes and adjustments may appear minor, yet make an exponential difference in terms of effectivness.

Summary

The objective throughout this book is to share the philosophies that Sensei Ota has developed throughout 40 years of study. We have attempted to show how those insights have evolved out of and further developed the Shorin-ryu lineage he inherited. We thought it was important to begin with Sensei Ota's direct lineage because it is that lineage, combined with his dedication and intense work ethic, that together have forged him into the Master that he has become. Sensei Ota's philosophy encompasses both the execution of body mechanics and the strategy that forms the basis for his practice of karate. We have endeavored to express that philosophy as it pertains to all aspects of the art, including kata, kumite and kobudo, as well as actual combat.

All great individuals throughout history tend to share one quality. They are driven to be the best they can be. People who achieve greatness are self-motivated; they tend not to be motivated by public spotlight or commercial success. They strive for their own standards of perfection, often without regard for the opinion of others. Sensei Ota is certainly such a man.

Sensei Ota is not concerned with gaining popularity or generating attention for himself. His commitment is purely to his art. It was for that reason, because he is so reserved about drawing attention to himself, that we felt that it was our responsibility, as loyal students, to tell his story for him, the story of a master of the art.

Summary

We hope the reader will indulge us in the shortcomings of this humble book and understand that any confusion or misinterpretation of Sensei Ota's philosophy in the text lies entirely with the authors. Our only defense is that it is sometimes difficult to translate martial philosophy into language.

Sensei Ota established his own organization in North America called the Shorin-ryu Karate and Kobudo Association. The goal of the organization is to increase awareness about Shorin-ryu karate in North America and to promote this beautiful and ancient style beyond the borders of Okinawa. Sensei Ota is committed to increasing the communication between Shorin-ryu practitioners in Okinawa and North America.

Many Okinawan karate and kobudo experts have difficulty with the English language, as well as sometimes formidable cultural barriers to overcome, and few have online Internet access. This is why an important objective of the organization is to help bridge this gap to increase the flow of information. Because Sensei Ota has lived in the United States for more than 30 years and can speak both Japanese and English, and because he is one of the most active senior Shorin-ryu practitioners, this responsibility has fallen upon him.

In addition to promoting Shorin-ryu and facilitating the greater exchange of information, Sensei Ota's mission is to introduce his unique training exercises and methodologies to help develop the body mechanics and strategy discussed in this comprehensive text. In this way, practitioners will hopefully increase their knowledge and enjoyment of karate and kobudo.

Sensei Ota can be found at **www.shorin-ryu.com**.

About The Authors

Michael Rovens

Mr. Rovens began training while in high school in San Francisco, California. Mr. Rovens moved to Los Angeles, California after earning a college degree at U.C. Berkeley, as well as a second-degree black belt in karate.

Michael searched for almost a year to find a new teacher. Finally a close family friend of Mr. Ota, who was coincidentally very friendly with Michael, recommended that he try Sensei Ota's dojo. Michael went to the dojo several times, but was not recognized or invited to join by either Sensei Ota or any of his students. Michael was instantly drawn to Sensei Ota and his style. So, finally he asked the mutual friend to intervene and was personally introduced to Sensei Ota. The entire conversation was held in Japanese, so Michael still does not know what was said. But finally after many sake, Sensei Ota got up and said, "Ok, you try tomorrow night." The next day Michael remembers taking off work early to purchase a new uniform with no crest and a white belt. Michael recalls thinking that this would demonstrate his commitment to Sensei Ota by showing that he was willing to begin with a "clean" mind. It also would show the obligation he felt to their mutual friend who put his reputation on the line for Michael. Mr. Rovens has been diligently trying to follow his Sensei ever since.

In 1988, Michael moved to New York after obtaining his MBA degree from USC to work on Wall Street. He left with the rank of first-degree black belt. Today, Mr. Rovens holds the title of Renshi, and is currently the highest rank, seventh-degree black belt, in Sensei Ota's organization.

Working on this book took Michael more than five years to complete. The effort, however, according to Mr. Rovens, was one of the most rewarding experiences he has ever enjoyed in martial

Michael Rovens (right) with Master Nagamine

Michael Rovens (right) with Master Shima

arts, particularly due to the countless hours spent with Sensei Ota going over every movement of every kata and every imaginable issue of strategy and how it relates to body mechanics and combat.

Michael also has studied Brazilian Ju-jitsu for many years and currently works full-time as an investment advisor for one of the top global investment banking firms.

Mark Polland

Mr. Polland dabbled in various forms of martial arts, including kenpo karate, tae kwon do, judo, and wing chun kung-fu before meeting Sensei Ota in the mid 1980s. According to Mr. Polland, it was only after he began studying with Sensei that his real training began. Since that time, he has frequently assisted with teaching classes at the dojo, as well as writing numerous articles about Sensei Ota and the Matsubayashi Shorinryu style of karate. In 2002, Sensei Ota promoted Mr. Polland to the rank of Go-dan, fifth-degree black belt. He continues to train with Sensei Ota on a weekly basis and refuses to live anyplace that is more than a 15 minute drive from Sensei Ota's dojo.

Mark Polland (left)

Mr. Polland says that, in addition to being a phenomenal athlete, Sensei Ota also has remarkable insight into other people. "All Sensei Ota has to do is see you walk across the room one time, and he knows everything he needs to know about you."

Besides his involvement in karate, Mr. Polland is also a full-time litigation attorney for a boutique law firm in downtown Los Angeles that specializes in construction law. He is also an accomplished fine artist, a university teacher and an avid outdoorsman with a passion for nature. At one time, Mr. Polland worked as a scuba diving guide in Central America.

Okinawan Karate

www.ingramcontent.com/pod-product-compliance
Lightning Source LLC
Chambersburg PA
CBHW081345080526
44588CB00016B/2377